GW00457987

I love Mexico
travel guide

By S. L. Giger as *SwissMiss on Tour*

"A journey is best measured in friends, rather than miles."
– Tim Cahill

Receive a free packing list

Never forget anything important ever again and don't waste unnecessary time with packing. Send an e-mail with the subject: **packing list** and receive a free packing list along with a sample of my Thailand travel guide.

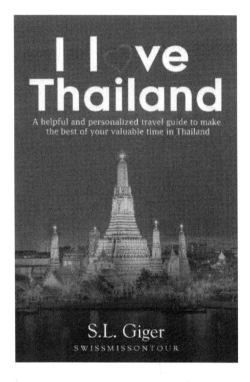

Send the e-mail to swissmissstories@gmail.com and receive your free gift.

Content

Why should I choose this guidebook instead of any other?

Do you only have a limited amount of time (like two or three weeks) and aren't quite sure which places of Mexico to fit into your schedule? Do you have doubts about whether it's safe to travel in Mexico or how to organize it best? This guidebook will help you to plan your trip and to really focus on the must-sees of beautiful Mexico. Prepare yourself for colorful houses, intensely blue waterfalls, and cenotes, delicious tacos, Caribbean beaches, and impressive ancient ruins.

Probably, the usual guidebook which talks about every small city will burst your timeframe. Therefore, you only find the best of the best in I love Mexico, which still could easily fill three weeks to a month, but you can also visit it in less time.

Do you want to plan your own, smooth journey in Mexico? This guidebook will make this an easy task.

Before my first trip to Mexico, I worried about the safety in the country. I thought I would get robbed or people would want to sell drugs to me and that I surely would be an easy target as a solo female traveler. So, I prepared myself with safety advice (which I also included in this book). My first trip was such a positive experience, that I returned as soon as I got the chance to spend more time in this diverse country. There is so much to see!

If you read this travel guide, you will get to experience the best of Mexico without having to do any further research. You find a two-week travel itinerary with detailed "how-to"-guidelines and further ideas and descriptions in case you want to spend more time in Mexico.

If you are worried about the Spanish language, there is a small language guide with helpful words at the end of this book. Otherwise, you should be fine with English and hands and feet.

Now, it's your turn to go exploring. Vamos!

Reasons to look forward to your journey in Mexico in case you are not entirely convinced yet

First things first; in case family members or friends who have never been to Mexico are warning you about the danger of traveling in Mexico, you can happily ignore their concern. I haven't felt unsafe in Mexico at all. On the contrary, locals are incredibly friendly and helpful. I'm not saying that there are no drug gangs in Mexico but normally, they are only a danger to each other and if a tourist gets caught in the middle it's a seldom and tragic accident. So, be assured that your trip to Mexico will only be filled with positive experiences and memories of all the amazing places that you will see. Because Mexico has a huge abundance of touristic sights to offer. There are the Mayan and Aztecan pyramids, wild monkeys in the jungle, clear freshwater that you can swim or dive in, white sandy beaches, and a lively atmosphere with Salsa music or other happy music that fills the streets. How could you be in a bad mood? It's easy to forget any kind of troubles in Mexico and just stare at beautiful nature in awe or feel relaxed.

Even while most of the countries were locked during Covid, Mexico welcomed travelers with open arms. I didn't have to present any kind of test upon arrival. However, that doesn't mean that they didn't respect hygiene. They were keeping everything clean, and you couldn't enter any entrance without someone splashing disinfectant on your hands or even spraying your whole body with disinfectant. Temperatures were measured everywhere as well. So, nobody can tell me that Mexico isn't doing a lot in order to keep the virus from spreading. Also, in the big cities, it's very easy to get tested. Often, there are medical tents in the streets, where you can get tested for around 20 USD for an antigen test and 100 USD for a PCR test. At the airport, you can get tested as well. With all those installations, I think they detect if someone is contagious and I felt very safe, even if places were crowded (for example Playa del Carmen or Cancun).

In conclusion, inform yourself about the current Covid situation of a country you want to visit (perhaps by contacting an airline) and then concentrate on not forgetting to bring enough sunscreen, mosquito repellent and your camera, to enjoy every minute in this wonderful country.

Mexico Highlights

Mexico is an explosion of colors. Be it waterfalls, the ocean, or buildings, the colors are more intense than in other countries. Apart from the amazing places you can see in Mexico, I think traveling in Mexico is also a lot about the social people you will meet. In no other country have I spontaneously spent time with strangers as much as in Mexico. Alexander Supertramp was right with "Happiness is only real when shared." And in Mexico, you will surely share your happiness with new friends.

1 Ek Balam Ruins

So many ruins are in Mexico that it's actually not fair to pick one as the best one. However, I really enjoyed Ek Balam because the ruins are surrounded by jungle and you could climb the steep steps up to the top, which gave way to a view across the jungle and the other ruins. Plus, there weren't as many tourists as in Palenque or Coba. Yet, I also liked Chichen Itza because it is so well preserved and Teotihuacan. After all, it's simply so big. Hence, I don't think you can travel to Mexico and only visit one archeological site :-).

2 Cenote Oxman, Valladolid

With the cenotes, it's the same as with the pyramids. There are so many and most of them are amazing. Cenotes are craters in the ground that are filled with underground water. Because the water is constantly filtered through rocks, it's incredibly clear and you can see as far as the light reaches. Plus, the water always shines in a light or dark blue. Some cenotes are connected through underground water passages that even lead into the ocean. Therefore, you find a mixture of sea and freshwater in some cenotes.

I loved cenote Oxman near Valladolid because tree roots hang from the ceiling down into the cenote. The crater is pretty open and therefore you have a lot of natural light, but the descent is cool because you follow along the crater wall. Other nice cenotes are Dos Ojos near Tulum, Jardin del Eden near Playa del Carmen or Santa Rosa in Homun.

In summary, if you want to have a bit of the best of all you should visit El Jardin del Eden for a nice open-air pool with trees and rocks, Dos Ojos for the blue color and the cave experience, and Oxman for the beauty of the vines.

3 Roberto Barrios waterfall

If this isn't your first travel guide by me, you might know that I love waterfalls! While the famous Agua Azul in the state of Chiapas certainly was pretty, I was even more struck by the just as blue Cascada Roberto Barrios. It's less touristy than Agua Azul, but there are many small waterfalls with ponds that you can swim in.

Things to consider before you visit Mexico to have the best possible trip

In this chapter, you find all the information for a smooth journey in Mexico.

Currency

Mexico uses the Mexican peso. The short form is MXN. However, usually, they put a dollar sign before the amount. So, if your fruit juice costs $20 it's actually about 0,80 USD because the $-sign doesn't mean USD but Mexican pesos.

In supermarkets, hostels, hotels, bus stations, and restaurants you can pay with a credit card or debit card. However, a lot of things you will buy from small street carts. Even for the entrance fees to archeological sites you mostly need cash. Therefore, try to bring small bills because often, they can't give you change.

At the time of writing this book, 1 USD equaled 20 pesos. So, to get the dollar price for the prices indicated in this travel guide, divide the number by 20. Mexico has been suffering from inflation in the past years and prices might be higher again soon. Therefore, check the momentary exchange rate by typing USD to MXN into Google.

Visa and Vaccinations

As I said, it was very easy to get into Mexico during both my trips (one before Covid and one during Covid). I neither needed a visa nor a vaccination. However, once you arrive in Mexico, you have to fill in an immigration card. Half of it, you will have to carry with you until you leave the country. Best tuck it safely inside your passport and don't lose it! The police might want to see it at random moments. There were checkpoints in Chiapas on the roads and they always looked in the vehicle very closely. I wonder what or whom they were looking for, but after I showed them my immigration card, they were happy and let us continue.

When I left Mexico, they tossed my card onto a pile with all the others at the airport. However, if I hadn't had my card, I would have had to pay a fine of about 40 USD. So, if you lose your immigration card, best go to a police station, and try to get a new one before leaving the country.

You can stay in Mexico as a tourist for up to 180 days.

Covid regulations

Because everything changes so quickly regarding Covid, I can't give you general travel advice for it. I strongly hope that by the time you are reading this book, Covid won't rule over the travel industry anymore. However, if Covid regulations are still in place, there are three things you need to check:

1. What regulations does Mexico currently have? Can your nationality enter the country? Do you need proof of a test or a vaccine? (Nothing was necessary at the time of writing this book.)

2. Are there any obligations when returning to your country? (You might need to get an antigen test or a PCR test and perhaps Mexico is on your countries quarantine list).

If you need an antigen test you can easily get it at CDMX airport. I contacted them via WhatsApp for an appointment, but it wasn't necessary. No other people were waiting when I got there at 9.30 a.m. It costs 650 pesos for an antigen test and you have to wait 30 minutes until you have the results. The PCR test costs 100 USD, and it will take 24 hours until you have the result.
You can get cheaper tests in the tents on the streets in Cancun or at Farmacias del Ahorro or Salud Digna. However, their PCR tests might take longer than 24 hours.

They checked my test result at check-in and then again at the security gate. After that not anymore.

3. Do you need a test or vaccine for the airline you are flying with or because of the stopover you are having?
Best contact the airline for information about that if you aren't sure.

If you fly inland in Mexico, you probably have to fill out an online health questionnaire. You can easily do that on your phone at the airport with the airport Wi-Fi. They will provide you with a QR code for the website.

Climate and the best time to travel

Mexico has a wet and a dry season. The dry season is from November to April and then it's great to travel anywhere in Mexico. In the rainy season, you can still visit most of Mexico, but you just have to expect a heavy shower once in a while. Also, from mid to end of the rainy season, it might not be worth visiting any "blue" waterfalls since they might be a muddy brown and dangerously strong.

Temperature-wise it's hot and humid all year long along the coast in the Yucatan area with temperatures being between 23°C and 35°C.

In the higher regions (for example Mexico City) it's usually a dry and warm 25-30°C during the day while temperatures fall during the night. While I was in CDMX in April, the range was between 13°C and 30°C, so I was glad to have long pants and a jacket in the morning but gladly wore shorts and a t-shirt later in the day. Either way, bring some warm clothes if you are planning to go to a city above 1500 m (like Oaxaca or San Cristobal de las Casas).

Drinking water and food safety

The tap water in Mexico is not safe to drink. Neither for tourists nor locals. You could suffer from severe stomach infections if you drink tap water. Therefore, buy filtered water or bring a travel water filter. I had my travel water filter with me to save plastic and went as far as even brushing my teeth with filtered water. That probably was a good idea because I didn't have any stomach problems (due to water) throughout my two trips to Mexico.

Sometimes, there are water dispensers or water filters in the accommodations, where you can fill up your bottles free of charge.

In the kitchen sink, you recognize the filter tap if, next to the faucet, there is a smaller faucet to which you can divert the water by turning a lever. This is the pipe for filtered water.

Since unfiltered water is bad even for Mexicans, they also use filtered water if they add it to fruit juice and for making ice cubes. Therefore, I think it's safe to drink fruit juices and cocktails. On top of that, you don't want to miss out on the delicious mango juices and margaritas.

The only foods you have to be careful with are raw vegetables and fruit that are washed in normal water. Hence, to really be safe from Montezuma's revenge, only eat raw food that needs to be pealed (like mangos or pineapples) or food that is cooked well.

Street food in Mexico is generally very safe. I ate from small street food carts the whole time that I was in Mexico and the only danger to my stomach was the extremely spicy sauces. Especially with raw seafood but also with cooked food, it's important that the food is fresh. Your chances of that are better if you eat at a place that is busy with other customers. I followed this rule strictly and only always ate where other locals were eating already.

With that in mind, I had a whole month in Mexico without the slightest stomach problem. Unfortunately, on my last evening, I went to a (busy) all-you-can-eat restaurant instead of a street taco cart. There must have been something bad in the food. I was puking for the next two days. On this occasion: I'm very sorry if you were sitting next to me on the plane!
Yet, let's not cloud the trip experience by this last memory. Traveling in Mexico is definitely enriching and fun.

How to stay safe in Mexico

Generally, I felt very safe in Mexico. It's easy to talk to locals and sometimes, we even traveled together for a while, if they were Mexican tourists who explored their own country. However, I am an experienced traveler, and, in a new place, I always keep my travel safety rules in the back of my head. You can read them below.

The only thing you really have to be careful with in Mexico is road traffic. In case you think walking along a highway instead of taking a taxi is a good idea, think twice. Cars drive extremely fast, and I have seen many people on the phone. One slip on the steering wheel and they would hit you.

Also, nowhere else have I seen so many tourists with scooter injuries as in Mexico. Not even in South East Asia, where scooter accidents are common as well. Keep that in mind and pay special attention whenever you are walking, riding a bicycle, or driving along a road. More than you would in your home country.

So, here is a list of 7 tips, how you can avoid getting yourself in a dangerous situation in any new country.

- **Spread your money**

Don't keep all your cards and money in one wallet. Spread them across several places of your luggage. Only always bring as much money as you think you will need for the time you will spend out of the accommodation. Perhaps, you withdrew 200 USD worth of pesos from an ATM but that doesn't mean that you will need it all in one day. Keep the rest somewhere safe.

- **Ask the locals about safety advice**

Locals know best how safe a place is. So, ask your hotel or hostel if you can hike to that waterfall by yourself or if it's okay to take a public bus to a certain place. If in doubt, I contacted my hostels beforehand whether it was safe to reach them by public transport or whether I should take a taxi. You can use Google Translate to translate your questions into Spanish or just see if they speak English.

- **Stay in populated areas**

It's more likely that you get robbed if you are the only person in an alley. Therefore, try to explore the parts of the town where other people are out and about as well. That being said, due to Covid, there were fewer people out and about. While visiting pyramids I sometimes was the only tourist for a while. However, there still were employed people around and I felt safe.

On the other hand, if you are in very crowded areas such as Zocalo in CDMX or the beach at Playa del Carmen, don't bring any valuables or never put them out of your hands.

- **Don't wear expensive jewelry**

Perhaps, I overdid this a little, but better safe than sorry. I left my finger ring at home and didn't wear my watch and only cheap plastic earrings. The best protection is if you don't present yourself as if you have money or as if you have something worth getting stolen.

- **Leave your passport and valuables in the hostel locker**

While sightseeing, perhaps carry around a picture of your passport on your phone and maybe bring your driver's license or another ID. I don't see a point in risking getting your passport stolen by a pickpocket. Especially at places like the beach, where you leave your things unattended, try not to bring anything of value.

- **Use Uber or Cabify**

In the big cities UBER, Cabify, and other taxi services are available. I found Cabify to be cheaper most of the time. These two taxi services are trackable which makes them safer. However, I often traveled by public colectivo or shared taxi in Mexico and it never was a problem.

- **Walk around with a plastic bag or cheap shopping bag**

Instead of an expensive-looking purse or camera bag, just bring your camera or anything else you carry with you in a cheap plastic bag. I traveled through South America with a free, reusable shopping bag and sometimes carried my laptop around in it while nobody would have expected that.

So, with those tips, I hope you will only experience the positive sides of Mexico.

How to avoid altitude sickness

Altitude sickness is no joke and can even put you in the hospital. You surely want to avoid a trip to a doctor or feeling lousy during your vacation. Altitude sickness can or can't affect anyone, no matter how fit, unfit, sportive, or lazy they are. It sometimes doesn't make sense who gets hit by it. If you arrive from sea level, you might already get out of breath while walking up a flight of stairs at 2000 m. If you arrive from a more elevated country, let's say 800 m in Austria, you will probably be fine at that elevation.

Mexico has several cities that are located at an altitude above 1500 m, for example, Mexico City (2240 m), San Cristobal de las Casas (2100 m), Puebla (2135 m), Guadalajara (1560 m), Oaxaca (1555 m).

For many people, 2000 m is the benchmark where they start feeling minor symptoms of altitude sickness. Unfortunately, some people even suffer gravely from it. Therefore, read the following information and tips carefully and you will hopefully pass your stay in Mexico without any kind of problems.

Symptoms of altitude sickness

It starts with dry skin and a dry throat. Any kind of exercise (walking stairs or a hill) will be much harder than it normally is and make you dizzy. Even turning around in bed could give you a racing heart. You could have a headache, and you'll probably feel bloated. If it gets really bad, you will feel sick and throw up. If you get a fever too or this lasts more than two days, see a doctor and try to get to a lower level of elevation. That is the best remedy anyway.

Tips to avoid altitude sickness

1. Stay hydrated

Especially if you arrive by plane, it's important that you drink three liters of water in 24 hours. The dry air on the plane dehydrates you and the high elevation does the same.

2. No alcohol on the first day (or even afterward, if you feel symptoms of altitude sickness)

Alcohol dehydrates you in addition to the dry air and if you feel dizzy already, it's not helpful to infuse your blood with alcohol.

3. Take it easy

Don't climb a mountain after a night bus or after arriving from a place at a lower altitude. Relax on your first day at a high altitude. Simply take leisurely walks around town. See how you're doing and then plan excursions for the following days.

4. Eat light

The altitude will squeeze your intestines together like a plastic bottle. Everything that doesn't fit will come out. So, in order not to feel sick, eat a small portion on the first day and perhaps don't start with a greasy burger and fries.

With these tips, you can hopefully enjoy Mexico City or San Cristobal without feeling sick. I wasn't affected by the altitude at all, but I heard some other people at the hostel in Mexico City talk about how they felt out of breath more quickly and one girl had a headache.

Traveling by bus in Mexico

Although flying within Mexico is very cheap, you will most likely still use several buses during your trip in Mexico. ADO has a bit of a monopoly on tourist buses. This is the recommended company for a comfortable and safe journey. The prices are usually higher than for other bus companies, but you always have an assigned seat with ADO, they have a/c, curtains, a toilet, a baggage compartment with a ticket system, and movies are playing on the big screens. Plus, the advantage of ADO is that you can look up the schedule on their website (www.ado.com.mx/). Sometimes, they have special discounts, especially if you book online in advance.

Bear in mind, that no snack vendors come onto the ADO buses. Buy your snacks ahead of your trip.

If you prefer paying less for a journey, ask around if there is a bus station for second class buses or if there is a colectivo. The disadvantage of cheaper means of transport is that there are no websites where you can check about their existence or what their schedule is. Plus, you don't have an assigned seat and sometimes you have to stand. This is uncomfortable if you have a big bag, and the journey is several hours long. In addition, buses for locals often stop at more stations and therefore take longer. Nevertheless, I have traveled with other companies than ADO (such as Oriente or Mayab) and I always arrived at my destination safely and well.

ADO bus or colectivo for traveling around?

You'd think that the colectivo taxis were cheaper than the bus as they are less comfortable to travel on them and they might stop or even wait along the way several times. Yet, at least in the Yucatan area, I found that ADO buses were often cheaper or the same price as colectivos. The colectivos are only better if you are on your own and no bus is going to that place or only a few connections. If you are three or more people, it might be cheaper to haggle down a taxi. Plus, if you travel with a big bag on the colectivo, they sometimes charge you extra.

How to keep safe and warm on the night bus

The buses in Mexico weren't as bad as in other countries in Latin America. However, often the night buses are cooled down a bit too much. Therefore, best bring something to cover yourself on a night bus (like a scarf or your towel) or wear long clothes.

Regarding safety, I didn't have any problems on my bus rides in Mexico. Yet, better keep your valuables on your body while you sleep. A money belt to hide your phone, the passport, and your wallet below your clothes is practical.

Finding your way

As everywhere I go, I used the *maps.me* app on my phone and downloaded Mexico for offline use. This has been a very useful companion every day and it always brought me to the place I wanted to go (for example, cenotes or a waterfall). You can use it to find points of interest within the city, to get to your accommodation, or to follow a hiking route. Tourists can mark spots and write comments and hence you can even discover secret spots which other tourists recommend.

Learn Spanish

In Mexico City and along the Caribbean coast, the locals are used to English-speaking tourists, and you should get along fine with English. Yet, it's friendly and useful if you speak a basic, touristy vocabulary of Spanish. The good news is that you really don't have to know a lot to get by. Yet, it has a big effect on the locals if you utter the first words you say to them in Spanish. They will appreciate your effort and quickly you become friends instead of strangers.

I first started learning Spanish with the free Duolingo app. However, I just didn't make any progress with it as there was so much unnecessary vocabulary that you simply don't need on a trip. Luckily, I then found **busuu**. First, you do a test that lets you start learning at exactly your Spanish level (after Duolingo I wasn't a complete beginner anymore), and the way it's set up makes the words and grammar sink in. I quickly became a fan and bought the premium program to access all the classes. This is a lot cheaper than taking a Spanish course and you can study while being on a plane or bus. I soon could follow conversations between locals. Speaking myself is still hard but it's nice to see that I am making progress every day.

Yet, the best option to learn a language still is to follow a course in the country where the language is spoken. Anywhere in Latin America, you will be able to find Spanish teachers (for example, through your hostel) to have private or small group lessons. So, in case you fall in love with a place, why not spend a few weeks there and practice Spanish?

Wi-Fi

All of our accommodations offered free Wi-Fi and many restaurants (not street food), and cafés provide Wi-Fi as well. Nowadays, the menus in restaurants are usually QR codes that you need to scan with your phone. Hence, they will give you Wi-Fi if you don't have your own data.

In CDMX there are free public Wi-Fi hotspots in many places. However, it wasn't very reliable.

There also was free Wi-Fi at all the airports.

In conclusion, I came by well without buying a local sim card or a data package.

Mexican food and drinks you need to try

Mexican food might not be the healthiest cuisine, but I absolutely love it. I could easily eat tacos every single day. There are so many different flavors to try and don't even let me get started about the sauces and other toppings. The salsas are so good, that I snacked tacos from different street food carts throughout the day, simply to try their version of salsa roja or salsa verde. However, when you order food, always ask if a sauce is spicy "piquante". Sometimes the red salsa is spicier and sometimes the green salsa. So, don't think just because you tried in one place, it will be the same in another.

Don't worry about not getting any toppings if you order takeaway food. They will pack salsa, onions, and whatever else you'd put on your food in small plastic bags so that you can add it later.

If you want something other than meat, your choice will be limited to cheese empanadas, beans, avocado, and cactus. The cactus is something you should try as well, as it is quite tasty! Other vegetables are difficult to find, therefore, try to get your vitamins with the delicious fresh fruit or shop on the market and cook yourself.

Here are some of the things you must try in Mexico:

- **Guacamole**

You probably know this delicious avocado mash from home already but of course, you have to try it in the country where this dish is from! They usually add onions and coriander to the guacamole, and sometimes small cut tomatoes. In a restaurant, they will serve you guacamole with chips. A normal serving is a big soup plate filled with

guacamole, which is meant to share. This costs between 80 and 100 pesos.

Yet, the restaurants adapted to the many single travelers in Mexico and it's often possible to get a half-serving of guacamole for half the price so that you can enjoy it alone.

- **Salty mango**

This is one of the most popular snacks you can find on the streets. They sell you the mango, shaved on a stick, inside a plastic bag. Then, they marinate it with a lime-flavored chili powder in front of your eyes. Add some spicy sauce, and voilà, you have your combination of sweet, salty, and spicy. I would leave out the spicy sauce, as it makes everything really messy. However, I found the combination of salt with mango very addictive, and Mexican mangos are delicious anyway. Most times, they cost 10 pesos.

- **Tacos**

Tacos are small, soft, round tortillas that are topped with all kinds of things (meat, fish, beans, vegetables). Then, you add even more toppings, like onions, cilantro, and sauces, you fold it together and eat it by hand. My favorite taco was "Al Pastor" which is thinly shaved pork meat mixed with onions and often topped with a thin slice of pineapple.

You can eat tacos in restaurants, but you can also buy them at taco carts along busy main roads and on parking lots. Prices start a t 7 pesos per taco up to 35 pesos per taco. Sometimes you can find promotions like 4 tacos for 35 pesos.

- **Empanadas**

This seems to be a breakfast dish as you often find empanada carts in the mornings. Mexican empanadas are deep-fried dough pockets filled with cheese, or meat, or beans, or a mixture of all of them. I prefer the fried Mexican empanadas to the baked empanadas from South America. Here in Mexico, they are more like Italian panzerotti. Quite addictive.

- **Quesadillas**

In Switzerland, the quesadilla is my favorite Mexican dish. Here, it is two tortillas that are stacked on top of each other. In between, they are filled with melted cheese, vegetables, and/or meat. Topped with guacamole or red salsa, it's a delicious combination of flavors. You can find this kind of quesadilla in the touristy parts of Mexico (like Cancun or Playa del Carmen). In other parts, something similar to this is called "Gringa". Because the usual quesadilla in Mexico is a bigger tortilla than what they use for a taco, that is topped with more ingredients than a taco and then you fold it or eat it with a knife and fork. So, the Mexican quesadillas aren't usually made with two tortillas, but the different vendors have their individual recipes for the tortilla flour, and you find quesadillas in all kinds of colors. The average price for one quesadilla is 40 pesos.

- **Churros**

This is a dessert or breakfast dish made of deep-fried sweet dough that is pressed into about 20 cm long, thin tubes. They are rolled in sugar or cinnamon and best consumed warm, while they are still crispy. You can dip them in chocolate or caramel as well. The average price for one churro is 8 pesos.

- **Ceviche**

Ceviche consists of raw or only quickly braised fish (usually white fish but you can also have it with clams and other types of seafood), lots of lime juice, onions, and cilantro. Most times, you then receive chips with it, to scoop the fish up with chips and eat it like this. Obviously, it's best if you eat ceviche in a seaside town where the fish is hopefully fresh. It's always a huge plate of fish and you won't be hungry for anything else if you order a ceviche. Prices start at 180 pesos.

- **Mezcal**

Like Tequila, Mezcal is made from the agave plant but stored in barrique barrels, which gives it a smokey flavor. Therefore, Mezcal should be sipped and enjoyed without mixing it with anything else. It's more like whiskey and it will warm your body from the inside. Enter a liquor shop to have a Mezcal tasting and find the flavor you like best.

- **Margarita**

This is my favorite cocktail since the combination of the salt rim on the glass with the cold mix of fruit, lime, and tequila is refreshing and sweet at the same time. The original margarita is with lime flavor, but they can also serve you mango, strawberry, and other flavors.

Often, they blend it with the ice, which in my opinion, alters the taste. Therefore, I always order "a las rocas" (on the rocks). You can find margaritas for 1 USD that are really good. Just stay away from ordering them at hostels or very touristy bars. There, I've only had very watery margaritas with artificial fruit flavor. The average price for a margarita is 5 USD.

- **Jamaica**

At all the street food carts you will see that you can buy some kind of iced tea as well. Sometimes, it's a white liquid, that is called horchata. It is made of rice or almond milk mixed with cinnamon and nuts. So, don't confuse it with coconut milk. You either like or hate the rice-cinnamon taste.
However, there also is a red iced tea that is called Jamaica. It is made of the Hibiscus flower and it's very delicious. On top of that, the sweetness gives you an energy boost on hot days.

How to pick your accommodation

Since travelers all have their individual preferences about what standard their accommodation needs to be, I seldomly include recommendations for hostels or hotels. The best deals for Mexico you get by booking all your accommodations on *booking.com* on genius level. There, you also have all the latest reviews for the hostels and can get an opinion about a place beforehand. Normally, I only book one night and if I like the place, I extend my stay. Of course, this doesn't work during local holidays and other special occasions.

If you want a more local experience, you should look for gems on *Airbnb*. Then, it's usually cheaper if you are several people and stay multiple nights.

Tips on how to find cheap flights to Mexico (and to any other country for that matter)

Luckily, often there are cheap flight deals to Cancun and even Mexico City. You can find return flights from Europe for as low as 350 EUR. From the US, the distance is shorter, and the flight prices are even lower. Here are seven tips to find the cheapest flight.

1. Use several flight search engines

I usually start looking for flights on **Skyscanner** and then I compare the deals from there with **Google flights**, **CheapTickets,** and/or **Opodo**. These sites tend to have the cheapest prices. Skyscanner for example, lets you set a price alert which will inform you with an e-mail when they have cheaper flights. You could do that half a year before your trip. In the end, I always check on the websites of my favorite airlines directly.

2. Be early and buy your flight at least 3 months in advance

If you know the dates of your vacation, there is no use to wait with booking your flights. They will only get more expensive.

However, during times of Covid, where everything is so uncertain, you are probably better off booking last minute. Otherwise, you might have to cancel your holiday if a country suddenly closes its borders again.

3. Be slightly flexible

Check the dates three days prior and after the dates, you chose to fly. There might be a huge price difference! If you search with the above-mentioned flight search engines it's very easy to have an overview of the flight prices on different dates.

4. Travel from other airports and book multi-leg flights

If you travel from Europe, it makes sense to check the airports in the surrounding countries and then buying a connecting flight from your country to get there. Cheaper airports to fly from are Munich, Frankfurt, Madrid, Amsterdam, Paris, Milan, and Brussels. However, this time, Zurich via Madrid with Iberia and checked-through bags was actually the cheapest for me.

If you fly from the US, often Miami and LAX are the cheapest.

So, if you have enough time, it's sometimes worth it to travel in several legs. Just calculate enough time in your connecting airport in case your first plane is delayed. You might have to go get your luggage and check it in for your new flight.

However, in times of Covid, you should opt for a direct flight if possible because every stop you make in between could mean more rules, more quarantine, or more tests.

5. Delete your browser history

The websites where you searched for your flight tickets to Mexico will recognize you on your second visit and raise the prices a little since you are still interested. So, if you notice an increase in the price, the first thing to do is to close the website, clear the browser history and then start searching again once you are ready to book. It's amazing how quickly you can save money this way.

6. Sign up for the newsletter from your favorite airlines

Newsletters still offer good value and often you find cheap airfares in them. At the moment, I regularly receive special offers from TUI and Iberia. By the way, SwissMissOnTour (www.swissmissontour.com) offers a newsletter as well. Sign up to receive my latest blog posts and a free and helpful packing list.

7. Flying cheap within Mexico

The cheapest airlines for Mexico are VivaAerobus and Volaris. However, they are only the cheapest if you fly with a small carry-on backpack and do without things like choosing a seat, food, and (with VivaAerobus) online check-in. Yet, they always transported me on time and without any issues.

If you have a bag that you need to check-in, buy the package at the beginning of the booking process. That will be cheaper than adding it later. At the airport, prices for checking in a bag are horrendous and they will surely weigh and measure your backpack if it looks big.

Two-week itinerary to see the best of culture and nature

Mexico has a lot of beauty to offer and wherever you go, you will hear about another place that you also need to visit. Therefore, it's difficult to squeeze all of Mexico in two weeks and you will need to fly inland. Yet, with the following route, you see the best of everything that Mexico is famous for.

Day 1: Arrival in Mexico City

Take a walk around the neighborhood of your hotel and Zocalo. Take it easy because of the altitude. Be sure to eat your first taco.

Day 2: Exploring the city

If it's a Sunday, you should go for a bike ride on Paseo Reforma. On any day, Parque Chapultepec is a nice place for a leisurely stroll and perhaps a visit to the zoo or the museum of anthropology. Head down to Coyoacan to see the colorful houses and have a fruit juice at the market. End your day in lively Roma.

Day 3: Trip to Teotihuacan

By bus, you travel one hour to the city of Teotihuacan. Take your time to stroll through the big ruins area. Then, return to CDMX. Perhaps you now have the time and energy to visit another neighborhood.

Day 4: Flight to Cancun and beach day

If you sit next to the window on the plane, try to spot a volcano from the air.

Now you have the choice of staying in a hotel in Cancun and enjoy the beach and nightlife in the *zona hotelera*. The advantage of Cancun is that there are small, surfable waves. If you are a surf fanatic and actually came to Mexico to surf, you will have to make a big cut out of this itinerary and travel to the Pacific Coast. There are many great surf spots anywhere between Puerto Escondido and Baja California.

If you don't want to surf, go to Playa del Carmen, and have some beach time there and enjoy the lively atmosphere.

Day 5: Cancun or Playa del Carmen

Have another relaxing day in this vacation paradise.

Day 6: Tulum and cenotes

Make your way to Tulum in the morning. If you don't have a lot of luggage, you can get off the colectivo at El Jardin del Eden cenote. The colectivo should be about 30 pesos to the cenote. In case you have a lot of luggage, you better leave it in Playa del Carmen and then return to get it, before continuing to Tulum.

After your first cenote, you can check on the map and decide whether you also want to visit Cenote Azul, which is right within walking distance of Jardin del Eden. Afterward, you continue to Tulum, where you can take a stroll along the main road to get a feel for this hip place.

Day 7: Tulum ruins and beach

Today, either travel by colectivo and then take a walk or rent a bicycle to get to the ruins in Tulum. Later you continue to Playa Santa Fe which is a picture-perfect Caribbean beach without any big hotels. Bring your towel and bathing suit.

Day 8: Valladolid and cenotes

Take the bus and 1.5 hours later you will be in one of the prettiest cities of Mexico. Drop your luggage off at the accommodation and then best rent a bicycle to head to Cenote Oxman, a pretty underground cenote with a big open roof. If you don't want to have to drive anywhere you could also visit Cenote Zaci in the center of town. Once temperatures cool down, take a walk around the pretty city center, and have dinner inside the market.

Day 9: Chichen Itza

Get up early and catch the first colectivo to go to Chichen Itza. For the first 30 minutes, you will have the place to yourselves without the tourist buses here yet. Marvel at the well-preserved ruins and once again be happy that you can be in such an amazing place.

After returning to Valladolid, you have more time to explore the city or go to another cenote. If you are up for more time on a bus, you could head to Izamal, the yellow city, for a couple of hours and then return to Valladolid in the evening.

Day 10: Rio Lagartos and Ek Balam

If you want to visit Rio Lagartos and Ek Balam in one day, you should rent a car with other people. If you are on your own, it's best to join a tour. Doing both places in one day without a car is possible and I will describe the tour for you in this travel guide but it's quite stressful. Nevertheless, both places are amazing as you will see pink water and flamingos at Rio Lagartos and can climb ruins in the jungle at Ek Balam. If you only want to visit Ek Balam, it's easy to go there by public bus.

Day 11: Bacalar and night bus to Palenque

Today is another packed day as you take a bus to Lake Bacalar in the morning (about 4 hours). Perhaps you can store your luggage at the ADO bus station or in a restaurant or hostel. Then, you have the whole afternoon to enjoy the blue hues of Lake Bacalar and take pictures pretending you are in the Maldives (bring your towel and bathing suit). In the evening, you take a night bus to Palenque, where you will arrive early in the morning.

Day 12: Roberto Barrios Waterfall

After the night bus, you probably don't operate on your full energy level. Then, you should take it easy and perhaps only spend half a day at Roberto Barrios Waterfall. The waterfall is one hour away from Palenque by colectivo. If you want to see more waterfalls and feel awake, you can join a tour that starts at 9 or 10 a.m. which visits the Palenque ruins, Misol-Ha, and Agua Azul.

Misol-Ha

Day 13: Palenque Ruins and flight to CDMX or Cancun

If you have done the ruins and waterfall tour yesterday, you can go to Roberto Barrios for half a day today, before taking the colectivo to Villahermosa airport. In case you have been at Roberto Barrios waterfall yesterday, you should take a colectivo to the Palenque ruins today, and then travel to Villahermosa for your (evening) flight. Unfortunately, there is no time to go down all the way to Agua Azul on the day of your flight. You should arrive in Mexico City around midnight.

Day 14: Flight back home

Hopefully, your return flight is not too early in the morning, so that you have time to sleep in and then eat one last taco before traveling home.

If your trip starts in Cancun, you follow this travel itinerary until Palenque from where you fly to Mexico City. One day before flying home, you return to Cancun.

Two weeks will feel like a long time with all the many things you will see, and you will have gained so much more from this vacation than by simply staying in the same place for 14 days. Now, let's have a closer look at the individual places.

Mexico City

Mexico City or CDMX (Ciudad de Mexico) as it is often called covers a big area with many individual neighborhoods. To see the various districts and their differences you will need several days in CDMX. However, you could spend weeks in Mexico City without being bored for a day. There are many great museums, ruins, street art, cool bars, colorful cafés, and of course, delicious street food. So, don't rush through Mexico City but take your time to see more than one neighborhood.

Also, Mexico City lies at an altitude of 2250 m. The altitude can affect your body and since you don't want to end up with a headache or feeling sick, follow the tips against altitude sickness in this travel guide. Plus, due to its location, it can get quite chilly when the sun is gone. You might appreciate long pants and a sweater in the mornings. I was in Mexico City in April, and it usually was 13 degrees in the morning, heating up to 30 degrees Celsius during the afternoon.

Now, that you have the right preparations for CDMX, let's have a look at how to get around the city and what to do.

How to get from the airport to the city center

The airport is located only about 8 km from the city center. Therefore, if you want it comfortable, take an UBER or Cabify for about 150 pesos (during the day). Probably, you will get stuck in a traffic jam for a while. At 5 a.m. from Zocalo to the airport, my UBER cost 70 pesos (15 minutes, no traffic) and at midnight it cost 90 pesos.

The cheapest option is the metro, which also only takes about 30 minutes to get to the city center and costs 5 pesos. You can buy a top-up card for 10 pesos that you can also use for the metro buses or you can always buy individual trips (then, you can't use the metro bus, but you can still use the normal public bus).

The metro is often very crowded so that you will be standing squished between other people. The doors close quickly so position yourself well when you want to get off. If you are female, I recommend that you ride in a car that is for females only. Just look for the designated pink area at any terminal.

To get to the metro station at the airport, you follow the sign that shows an "m" with a line on top of it. Since the exit area of the airport is really long, it might take you up to 20 minutes until you reach the metro station. For the last 3 minutes, you leave the airport building and walk along a covered outdoor path.

To get to the center you ride in the direction of **Pantitlan** (I had to take the underpass to the opposite track). At Pantitlan you switch onto the pink line number 1 which brings you into the city center. For **Zocalo,** you switch to the blue line at **Pino Suarez**.

Traveling around the city

The easiest (but not always the quickest way) is by metro. Take a picture of the metro map in a metro station and afterward, you can check on that picture which connection you need to take. This way, you don't always have to look for a metro map first. If you have mobile data, you can of course check for the best connection on Google.

Then, there is the metro bus which travels on overpass-ways in straight lines. For the Metrobus, you need a touch card. Most trips cost 7 pesos. If your destination is along a Metrobus line it will be quicker than the hassle with the subway. Plus, you will have a seat.

There are different waiting zones at the Metrobus terminals, and you need to bord there where the final destination of your bus line is written at the top.

Thirdly, there are other public buses that run in 2-minute intervals. The destination and some important stops are marked in the front. If it says where you need to go, hop on. A ride costs 4 pesos and you need exact change or a Metrobus card.

If in doubt, tired of walking, or after midnight you can always order an Uber.

What to do in Mexico City

The things to do in Mexico City are as diverse as its neighborhoods. However, don't expect early mornings. You won't even find a street vendor before 7.30 a.m. Cafés open at 8 a.m. even if it says earlier on their website and museums open between 9 and 11 a.m. So, enjoy your party the night before, sleep in, and then go sightseeing in the rhythm of the Mexicans. Here are the must-do activities for CDMX:

Zócalo

This is the historic center of the city, and as in most Latin American cities, it is located around a big square. Take pictures of the big Mexican flag or the pretty colonial buildings and the Metropolitan Cathedral that surround the square.

Must-see places in Zócalo are the *House of Tiles* (which is a beautiful building of which the facade is made entirely of blue painted tiles). Further, you might like the big *Palacio de Bellas Artes*. It is a pretty building and also hosts cultural events, including a permanent art museum. For more information go to their website or take a virtual tour there: http://museopalaciodebellasartes.gob.mx/. Entry to the museum is free on Sundays.

For a lively atmosphere and bars with music, head to *Regina Street* (this is the place to go out in the evening if you aren't going to Roma). In addition, there are beautiful murals along Regina Street, so don't forget to look up.

Another interesting spot in Zócalo is the area where you can see entire units of the *Tenochtitlan* ruins. Some pillars can even be seen inside the Zócalo metro station. You can have a look at parts of the ruins from above without paying or you can enter the *Templo Mayor Museum*. It costs 70 pesos and is free on Sundays.

Apart from looking at historical things, you can go shopping in a wide range of modern shops in Zócalo.

Reforma

On Sundays, one of the biggest streets in CDMX, *Paseo de la Reforma* is closed for cars from 8 a.m. to 2 p.m. The closed part stretches from the top end of Parque Chapultepec for 12 km to past Hidalgo metro station.

It's a beautiful atmosphere to walk, jog or ride a bicycle among locals. You can get up close to the Angel of Independence, that is situated in the center of a big roundabout. You can even borrow free bikes from the government. They hand them out from small huts along the road that look like kiosks starting at 10 a.m. You can rent the bike for 3 hours if you hand them an official ID that has an expiry date in the future. Enjoy your ride!

If it's not a Sunday, this area still offers many shops and restaurants, but the streets will be busy with cars. Most of the big hotel chains are located along Paseo de la Reforma and simply by following this busy road you will discover pretty sights like the *Revolution Monument* and some important skyscrapers.

Also within walking distance of Paseo de la Reforma you will land in *Zona Rosa*. It received its name because there are many rose-colored buildings in this neighborhood but it's also the center of the LGBT-friendly community. However, anybody is welcome, and people like to come here to shop or go out, especially along Calle Amberes and Calle Florencia.

Parque Chapultepec

In a huge city like CDMX, you are glad if you can escape to a green space from time to time. Parque Chapultepec makes this very easy as it is reachable by metro or by bus and you could spend a whole day in the park as it is so big and there are so many things to do. For example, you could visit **Castle Chapultepec**, which has beautifully colored

windows. It costs 80 pesos to enter.

Across the road from the park is the **Museum of Anthropology**, which many people like. It also costs 80 pesos to enter. Then, there are lakes where you could paddle around on a boat or you could join one of the sports classes that take place in the park. In addition, there are many vendors along the main road through the park and on weekends it seems like a gigantic street festival that guides you to the zoo.

Zoológico

CDMX has several zoos and the one in Parque Chapultepec is sponsored by the government. Since they want to make it accessible for everyone, entry is free. This doesn't mean that you find a small pet zoo with farm animals. No, there are orangutans, big cats, and even pandas! Since there are only a few zoos in the world that breed pandas, this is a good opportunity to see these cute animals in reality.

Condensa

This was my favorite neighborhood because it was lively but clean at the same time, and if you want an even bigger choice of bars, you can cross over into Roma on foot.

Dance Salsa or Bachata

On weekends there is a Salsa or Bachata class in *Parque Mexico* from around 1 p.m. under the covered arch. After that, they keep dancing. Parque Mexico is an awesome place to be at the weekend anyway as lots of people are doing sports there and there always is something interesting to watch.

Roma

This is a lively neighborhood with charming bars, nice restaurants, and colorful buildings. This is the go-to neighborhood if you want to go out at night.

It's also nice to stroll through the parks and look at the fountains and statues. For a local food experience head to the colorful *Mercado Medellín* and enjoy a cheap, fresh fruit juice. Usually, they don't add water to juices, so your stomach should be fine, and your body will appreciate the dose of fresh vitamins. *Mercado Roma* is a more modern, expensive, and touristy food hall but also nice to visit.

Along the busy road where the metro buses drive you find street vendors selling delicious and cheap tacos, quesadillas, etc.

Coyoacan

This neighborhood is a bit further away from the others and the metro ride to get here from the center takes about 30 minutes. In Coyoacan you can see the most colorful houses of CDMX. Around the square with the **Fountain of the Coyotes,** you might even feel as if you landed in earlier times. Take a stroll through the neighborhood (on which you really shouldn't miss the fountain with the two playing coyotes

and the local market). Perhaps you want to pay a visit to the *Frida Kahlo Museum* which is located in a blue building. It's a bit more expensive at 230 pesos (weekdays)/ 270 pesos (weekends) and maybe it's a good idea if you take a virtual tour on their website before you go (www.museofridakahlo.org.mx/en/the-blue-house/ your-visit/#back-top). Another point of interest in this area is the *Leon Trotsky Museum* (museocasadeleontrotsky.blogspot.com/) which is located in a red building. It's the original house where Leon Trotsky lived in 1940 and was murdered.

Good for a local experience is *Coyoacan Market*. Take a break from your walk and have a delicious fruit juice (the small glass is 0.5 liter and costs 20 pesos) or buy some snacks.

Polanco

This is the posh neighborhood, and you might even think for a moment that you are in Beverley Hills. Enjoy a coffee and some churros while looking at beautiful houses and people or shop at luxury brand stores.

Where to stay in Mexico City

Since the neighborhoods are so different, you should choose an accommodation according to where you want to spend most of your time. The rest is easily accessible by public transport or Uber. However, if you are looking for a blissful oasis in the middle of busy CDMX stay at the following hotel:

Four Seasons Mexico City

If you want to treat yourself to a relaxing stay in a beautiful environment, look no further. The Four Seasons Hotel is a beautiful green oasis in busy CDMX. The design alone with the big green courtyard and the picturesquely decorated restaurant and bar make you feel calm and in a holiday mood. The small pool on the terrace of the third floor is a great place to escape the hot temperatures and relax your sore feet after visiting the city. If you still haven't had enough exercise, you can work out in the modern and well-equipped gym. But let's get back to relaxation: The bedroom is spacious with a lot of natural light from the big windows and the pillows and sheets are so comfortable that I slept really well. Also, it was very quiet! I haven't found another accommodation in CDMX without any noise.

The only downside that I can think of is that food prices inside the hotel are almost Swiss, whereas you can eat in the local restaurants around the hotel for a fraction of the hotel prices. Not even the coffee in the room was free, which I haven't experienced in any other hotel. But apart from that, I would stay at Four Seasons anytime again as everything else brought me directly to a blissful paradise.

Day trip from Mexico City: Visit the famous ruins of Teotihuacan

The latest by now you know that Tenochtitlan and Teotihuacan are in fact two different ruins and not just a spelling error. If you see pictures of big pyramids which you can climb, you are looking at Teotihuacan. Those pyramids are located 1 hour from the city center.

How to get to Teotihuacan

There really is no need to join a tour as it is easily accessible by public transport and the tours usually take much longer than needed because you ride around to collect the other guests.

Take blue bus 1 from the city center or metro line 5 to **Terminal de Norte**. Check on Google for your best connection. If the blue bus doesn't arrive in 3-5 minutes, ask a local for the correct bus to Terminal de Norte. Sometimes, the bus stops get moved around the corner as it was in my case.

At Terminal de Norte you buy your ticket to Teotihuacan from the booth next to window 8. If you can't pronounce the name of the city, just say "piramides". Buses leave every 30 minutes. Mine left at 9 a.m. You buy a return ticket for 104 pesos. The last return bus is at 8 p.m. During the journey, you see colorful houses and many hills. The ride took 50 minutes and they dropped me off at the parking lot in front of gate 1. I walked to the ticket booth and bought the ticket for 80 pesos. Amazing if you think that such a well-preserved historical area only costs 4 USD to visit.

Visiting the pyramids

It took me 1 h 45 minutes for visiting the pyramids without a guide and without climbing them. Unfortunately, due to covid you couldn't climb the pyramids or enter the chambers near the Pyramid of the Moon. Of course, this is a pity if you are only here once in your life, but the visit was still worth it. The huge area of the ruins is impressive on its own and it was probably even more special to see the pyramids without people on them.

If everything is open, you probably need 3 hours for your visit. In order to fully enjoy the walk, best wear a big hat (you can even buy one at the entrance for 50 or 100 pesos if you haggle a bit), lots of sun protection, and, perhaps, bring an umbrella to shade yourself from the sun. You are completely exposed to the sun the whole time and the light that reflects from the rocks in the archeological area makes it even hotter. Therefore, bring at least a liter of water for your visit, too.

Afterward, you can get the return bus to Terminal de Norte from the 2nd gate near the Pyramid of the Moon. So, there is no need to walk the 2 km back to the entrance gate.

This time the journey to CDMX took 1 h 10 min because we first drove through the village of Teotihuacan. Hence, you could also walk or take a taxi into the village and eat something at one of the restaurants before returning to CDMX.

Cancun

From Europe, the cheapest flights will bring you to CDMX or Cancun. If you want to see both places, book a cheap inland flight with VivaAerobus or Volaris. The two-hour flight can be as cheap as 25 USD and if you are lucky, you will see some volcanos out of the plane window.

Now, let's talk more about Cancun. You might have already heard of this but frankly, Cancun is nothing pretty. It's like Mallorca's Ballermann for Americans and even the beaches of the all-inclusive resorts don't look so tempting. There always only is a short stretch of sand which is crowded with many beach chairs. Hence, I would recommend using your time in Mexico to visit the colorful towns and ancient ruins with perhaps only one or two days at a beach in order to stop your craving for the ocean. That being said, I enjoyed my stay in the Zona Hotelera of Cancun very much but mostly because of the amazing hostel I stayed at and the friendly people there.

How to get to Cancun Center or the hotel zone

From Cancun airport take an ADO bus to the city center for 98 pesos or share a taxi, and then switch on the R1 or R2 minibus from the corner at the main road near the ADO station. R1 and R2 buses drive along the hotel zone every minute and one ride costs 12 pesos.

What to do in Cancun

In the city center, there wasn't anything going on because of covid. Plus, the center isn't at a beach and there aren't really any sights, so, it's best you make your way to the hotel zone or even to another town quickly.

Stay at Mayan Monkey Hostel

This hostel is located on a platform above the lagoon. From comfortable chairs or swings, you have a pretty view across the lagoon while chatting to new friends you meet at the hostel. Sometimes a big crocodile swims by (yes, the warning signs aren't just for show). The hostel was clean, and the rooms were well insulated so that it was quiet even when there was music in the main area. I had some of my best nights of sleep there of all of my stays in Mexico.

Right across the road of the hostel, there is a beach access path and in one minute you are at the ocean. Plus, there are free wooden beach umbrellas which make it easy to stay at the beach all day without getting burned.

Fill your belly with empanadas or tacos

You can find cheap street food in the tiny ally behind Mercado Coral Negro. There are always locals eating at the food stalls. If it's too hot for you to eat next to the cooking stations, there is one place where you can sit down adjacent to the market inside a shop. I liked their empanadas and tacos which you could decorate with the available toppings. Food items cost between 20 and 40 pesos.

Party until you drop

Most people go to Cancun for parties. Be prepared for a mix of really loud music that roars out of all the discos. If that and cheap alcohol (not particularly good cocktails) sound like your scene, you will feel right at home.

Surf

Cancun really isn't the best place for surfing and if you know what you are doing better go to the West Coast, for example, small towns near Puerto Escondido or Baja California. However, if you just really miss the feeling of the waves, you will also have some fun on a board in Cancun. There was a surf school opposite of the Mayan Monkey hostel, where you could rent boards. Apart from that a surf instructor was renting out boards and giving lessons at the beach umbrellas at Chacmool Beach. You could rent boards starting at 300 pesos per hour, but you can haggle a bit and if you take it for longer or several days it will be cheaper as well. I heard the best surf is at Playa Delfines, which also looks like a rather nice beach. However, because it's quite far South in the Hotel Zone and the heat can make you tired, I only visited the beaches between the start of the hotel zone and *La Isla Mall*.

Go shopping

Speaking of La Isla Mall, in case you want to cool off from the beach, you can stroll through the shops or restaurants at this nicely designed mall with many shaded outdoor areas.

Eat ceviche

In any town along the coast, you should eat this delicious dish. It consists of shrimp or fish that was marinated in lime juice. The portions are big and plenty for sharing. You can find a good price-value ratio at *La Bamba Seafood*. It's a small place next to the *Surfin Burrito*.

Playa del Carmen

Playa del Carmen is another famous beach and party town on the Caribbean coast. I loved the atmosphere in this lively town during all my visits. It's like a never-ending street festival. In addition, you find cheaper food and drink prices than in Cancun. Unfortunately, in 2021 the beach was dirty with seaweed and therefore not so nice to look at. Plus, you swim near the ferry terminal to Cozumel, so I don't know how clean the water is. On the other hand, there are fewer skyscrapers in Playa than in Cancun and you can find a place to dance Salsa almost every day of the week.

How to get to Playa del Carmen

Either take a comfortable ADO bus from the airport or downtown Cancun for between 36 and 80 pesos or take a colectivo van (also with a/c) opposite the entrance to the downtown ADO terminal for 45 pesos. The journey in either vehicle takes 1 hour.

Be aware that there are two ADO stations and many colectivo stops in Playa del Carmen. So, have your map ready to find your hotel once you get off.

What to do in Playa del Carmen

You can do anything beach-related from just relaxing to getting married. Simply strolling along Calle 5, buying some souvenirs, and sitting down in a colorful restaurant or café can fill several days and evenings. By the way, the souvenir shops with big discount signs really have the best prices in Mexico. You can buy a pretty Mexican blanket for as low as 3 USD.

Dance Salsa or Bachata

On Friday nights, the *Selina hostel* hosts a salsa and bachata party with professional lessons before that. Of course, that depends on the teachers. During my visit, there was a beginner level and an advanced level, and we learned awesome moves. Funnily, they were teachers from Azucar Abasto in Buenos Aires, where I had also been dancing during my South America trip :-).

Ladies drink for free

You will find enough places to drink and party in Playa to fill your week. The most fun thing for women is to check out lady's night. You will see signs on bars or hostels announcing it. I was at one where it said "ladies drink free until 10 p.m.". And really, I did not have to pay for any of my cocktails. Plus, it was one of the best Margaritas I had in Mexico.

Get a massage

You can find massages at the beach for 20 USD and anything above that.

Visit some cenotes

The best cenotes near Playa del Carmen are easily reachable by colectivo. Simply take the colectivo toward Tulum and tell the driver that you want to get off at **El Jardin del Eden**. The colectivo should cost about 30 pesos and will take 20 minutes. At the stop, you have to walk about 15 minutes to get to the water. This was the first cenote I visited (200 pesos) and afterward, I wanted to see more. El Jardin del Eden is a big open-air cenote. The water is green but very clear and you can jump from the rocks on one side.

It is closed on Saturdays. Best ask your accommodation about current opening times of cenotes in case something changed.

Cenote Azul

This cenote is a few minutes walking distance from Jardin del Eden. There are different shallow creeks. One is blue and the others are rather green but all very clear. It was a bit like how I imagine paradise to be but with more people. The entry fee is 100 pesos.

Where to eat in Playa del Carmen

There are many nice-looking tourist restaurants in Playa del Carmen, and you can find many kinds of cuisines. On some evenings, they have special promotions (for example, 2x1 sushi rolls on Thursdays), where you can eat cheap and delicious sushi.

If you want authentic Mexican food, look for empanada or taco carts in the mornings or evenings along the main traffic avenues. If you want to sit down in a restaurant, go to "Taquerias El Sabrosito del Fogon" between Old Navy and the square with the statues. The restaurant is upstairs, where you have a nice breeze from the ocean. The prices are fair, and the food is delicious.

If you want to cook yourself, there is a big Walmart.

Leaving Playa del Carmen

You can either continue along the coast to Tulum (colectivo: 45 pesos/ADO: 98 pesos, 1 hr), or inland to Valladolid (ADO: 276 pesos, 2.5 hrs), or Merida (direct ADO bus for 550 pesos, 4 hours or a cheaper Mayab express that will take 6 to 9 hours). Make sure that you know from which terminal your bus is leaving - not that you wait at the wrong one and your bus leaves without you.

Scuba diving from Cozumel Island

My parents have visited Cozumel on a cruise and became instant fans. They spent their day in a pretty beach club with a white beach and all-inclusive alcohol. Sounds good, right?

Well, I then traveled from Playa del Carmen to Cozumel by ferry because I wanted to go scuba diving. My experience was a bit different. Therefore, read on to find out why I wouldn't necessarily recommend leaving mainland Mexico and spend precious time on Cozumel which you could rather spend at another location.

How to get to Cozumel

This is easy. Walk to the ferry terminal in the city center of Playa del Carmen (or take a taxi there). The companies are Winjet (https://winjet.mx/eng/) and Ultramar (www.ultramarferry.com/en/routes-and-departures) and they leave almost every hour between 8 a.m. and 9 p.m. A return ticket costs 25 USD (a bit cheaper if you buy it at the counter in pesos) and the ride takes about 45 minutes.

The beaches on Cozumel

Once you arrive on Cozumel, you realize that not the whole island is surrounded by soft, white beaches but there are quite a few rocky spots. However, Cozumel is too big to explore on foot. Hence, you either rent a bicycle and ride in the hot sun, take a taxi, or rent a car to get to a free public beach. The better option is to pay the entry fee to a beach club. Usually, you receive a snack or drink with your entry fee. With all this trouble, you might just as well stay on mainland Mexico, where you can find nice beaches as well.

Diving on Cozumel

The underwater world around Cozumel is diverse. Therefore, it's a nice area for scuba diving. Two dives cost about 90 USD. Unfortunately, I was a bit unlucky with my company. It took a long time until they had all the equipment sorted out although we were only three guests. They seemed to be very disorganized. After our second dive, we then heard that another group lost a diver and so we all stayed out with the boats to go look for him. That's so dangerous and I couldn't believe that this actually happened! In the end, they found him after an hour, and it ended well. However, I did not join a second day of diving and was looking forward to getting back to Playa del Carmen.

Experience island life on Isla Holbox

Holbox (pronounced: Holbosh) is still a paradise island where you walk barefoot in white sand and spend your days on beautiful beaches, sipping out of coconuts or hanging in hammocks. If you have time (for example, if you cut out Palenque of the two-week itinerary, since it's a bit far to travel there), definitely take the trip to Holbox and spend a night or two on the car-free island. In the evening you have the amazing chance to see fluorescent plankton. Maybe, the water is already glowing in a blue hue when it rolls up onto the beach. If not, stand into knee-deep water and swirl your hands around after sunset. If plankton is present, there will be a glowing halo around your hand.

How to get to Isla Holbox

The ferries leave from the small town of Chiquila. You can get there by ADO bus from Cancun or Playa del Carmen (each about 2 h 30 mins, approximately 290 pesos) or by colectivo (same duration, about 250 pesos). The ferries leave every 30 minutes, and you buy the ticket at the dock. One-way costs 200 pesos and takes 30 minutes.

Tulum

When I was in Tulum four years ago, it had a calm, artsy vibe. On top of that, there are rest-aurants with good food, a picture-perfect Caribbean beach with white sand, and many stunning Cenotes. Of course, all the good things are still there. It simply got a bit busier over the years and turned into a bit of a hipster place (similar to what happened in Kuta on Bali). Hence, Tulum definitely isn't a secret tip anymore. Yet, all the pretty sights around Tulum, especially the ruins by the sea, make it inevitable to spend a few nights or even longer in Tulum.

How to get to Tulum

You can reach Tulum from all the cities in the Yucatan area along the coast, for example, by colectivo or ADO from Playa del Carmen (1h, 40 pesos). From Cancun via Playa del Carmen with two colectivos or one ADO bus (2h 40 min, 198 pesos), from Bacalar by ADO (2h 50 min, 304 pesos) or Valladolid by ADO or Mayab (1.5h, 130 pesos).

Things to do in Tulum

Tulum has something for everyone. However, apart from free street art, be prepared to pay higher entry fees for tourist sites than in other cities.

How to visit the Tulum ruins without a tour

To get to the Tulum ruins from Tulum you have three options. Either you drive your own car, you ride a bicycle, or you take a colectivo.

- The bicycle rent is about 150 pesos per day. You cycle along the road back toward Playa del Carmen for about 4 km. There is a bike path and so it should be pretty safe. Many people are doing it this way and it's a good option to get past the traffic jam. Then you see a big sign "zona archeologica Tulum" and there you turn right. There is a car park to the right as well but with the bike, you can cycle on for about five hundred meters to the entrance.
- With your own car, you follow the same route but stop at the parking lot.
- By colectivo: They stop along the main road close to the ADO terminal. Just approach one that is waiting or flag one down on the roadside where you drive to Playa del Carmen. If you can't find them although it's easy ask about "colectivo para las ruinas". To make sure, ask the driver "Tulum ruinas" or "zona archeologica" when you get on. The ride should take about 10 mins (but it can take

anything up to 1 hour with the new traffic jam), and the driver will yell "zona archeologica" when you arrive (approximately 15 pesos). Like the ones who came by car you now have to walk along the boardwalk with all the other tourists for about 500 meters. There are many vendors along the way. If you are really tired you could also take a tourist train to the entrance.

Visiting the Tulum Ruins

The entrance fee is 70 pesos which is cheap compared to everything else in this area.

Perhaps the ruins are not as impressive in height as other ones, but they are cool because they are built on a cliff and you can take lovely pictures with the ocean in the background. Be sure to take a swim at the white sandy beach in front of the ruins as it gives you another amazing view of them!

The fun thing is that you will spot about 1000 iguanas in all sizes and colors during your visit. They are quite curious as well and move around or even check out your stuff on the beach. So, be sure to close your bag when you go into the water :-).

Playa de Santa Fe

This was one of my favorite beaches ever as it was just so beautiful with the white sand, palm trees, and different shades of blue water. "Too nice to even pee in it" as my Mexican friend said to me.

The sad thing was that there was a lot of seaweed during February and March (this problem started in 2015 as a side effect of global warming). There was one bar to get ice cream along the beach and the ice cream was absolutely delicious.

To get to Playa Santa Fe you can walk 15 more minutes from the entrance or exit of the ruins along the road that goes parallel to the ocean. You can also bike there and leave the bicycle at the entrance to the beach.
If you come straight from Tulum, you will arrive from the other direction at the same road that runs parallel to the ocean. It's also possible to come by colectivo but you will

 have to walk quite far. In addition, all the passing colectivos when I wanted to return were full and I had to wait quite a while.

By the way, you can never say to a taxi to take you to "playa" as they will drive you to Playa del Carmen instead of the closest beach. Happened to a French friend.

Diving in a cenote

There are also various cenotes spread around Tulum. Some are within cycling distance, but most of them are too difficult to reach if you don't have a car or don't join a tour. Therefore, if you don't have a rental car, I'd recommend going scuba diving in the cenotes. That way, you will be shuttled to the cool cenote and probably still have time to check out the rest of the cenote while you aren't diving. Another option is to take a taxi to the cenote or join a cenote snorkeling tour in case you don't scuba dive.

In my opinion, the must-see cenote in this area is *Dos Ojos*. It consists of two ponds and the colors when the sun is shining are amazing. Even with snorkeling, you can see many stalagmites and stalactites. The second "eye" is much better than the first one, so you should spend more time there. Once you are done swimming, you can find hammocks at the top and bathrooms and showers. The only downside is that it's quite expensive at 350 pesos.

Scuba diving in a cenote

I went diving in The Pit and Dos Ojos for 130 USD including transport, the entry fees, and a fruit lunch. It's an expensive diving area but the experience is worth it. There are many dive schools offering cenote trips. You will find one that suits you if you walk along the main road in Tulum.

The Pit

The Pit was our first dive as it is a deep dive and only open to Advanced divers. To get to the cenote you have to climb down (and then back up) a steep wooden stairway (with the heavy equipment) but we were rewarded with being the only ones in the cenote except for a group of divers that was already under the surface. It was amazing to later see them 30 m away from us in the dark blue water. The water is incredibly clear and just gets a darker shade of blue the deeper you go.

It looks nice when the sun rays enter through the water from the top. We saw interesting stalactite formations, the colors on the wall of a former waterfall, and the skull and bones of a monkey.

At 30 meters depth, there should be a white fog due to the salt and freshwater meeting and in the middle of it there is a tree (without leaves). It looked nice although the fog was only slightly visible on that day. But the water texture did become a bit different as if it were mixed with oil.

As it can be kind of dark in the caverns you are obliged to have a flashlight on all the cenote dives. Sometimes, we covered the light and just enjoyed the true colors from the cenote changing from the surface to the blackness below us (The Pit is about 130 m deep).

As we surfaced again, we were met by a few bats and then ate our fresh fruit lunch in the sunshine.

Scuba Diving at Dos Ojos

This dive was even better than The Pit and should not be missed! We did the Barbie Line. It has its name due to a barbie that they drowned at the turning point of the under-water line. She ended up in the mouth of a plastic crocodile.

At the beginning of the dive, we were with many other divers as well as the snorkelers. However, I think they all made the Bat Cave line since afterward we were completely alone on the dive. We saw lots of interesting formations, but the nicest thing is to see the sunlight from above. It really shows all the different shades of blue. The whole time you follow a thread below the surface. Probably better as you might lose yourself in one of the caverns otherwise.

Dreamgate

Diving at Dreamgate would have been our third choice. It's supposed to be stunning as well with all its formations.

However, it's a cavern dive completely in the dark. I don't think I'd have liked it as much as Dos Ojos. The Pit and Dos Ojos could be pretty dark at times as well but what I loved about them was when the sunlight changed the colors underwater.

Secret beach tip

Xcacel Beach lies a 20 minutes' drive north of Tulum and is not well known yet. You can easily get there by colectivo toward Playa del Carmen. You pay a donation and can enter a beautiful beach which you have almost to your-self and a small cenote on top of that.

Snorkel with turtles

Akumal is the place to snorkel with turtles but I didn't see one when I was there in February. Perhaps it's better around their hatching season between May and

November. You can also get to Akumal by colectivo between Playa del Carmen and Tulum.

Where to eat in Tulum

All my favorite restaurants are located on the main road of Tulum at the end toward Chetumal.

You absolutely have to eat at *Antojitos la Chiapaneca* (the orange restaurant at the end of Tulum toward Chetumal on the right side). They have a lump big kebab meat in front and the restaurant is always packed with people. I recommend anything "Al Pastor". They have tacos, empanadas, tortas and panuchos or quesadillas all for 8 pesos or 12 pesos with cheese (con queso). You can choose many toppings if you eat in the restaurant and otherwise, they will pack you some for takeaway. Careful, the spicy sauce is REALLY spicy.

Burrito Amor

This is a hip place with a nice ambiance and sometimes live music. Plus, the burritos are good and served in banana leaves. The rest of the food and the drinks are healthy as well.

La Barracuda

My hostel said that this is the only place that actually has fresh seafood. The ceviche is good and so big that you can easily share a small one with a side of Guacamole. The cocktails aren't strong, but beer is always good.

Muyil float in the Sian Ka'an reserve

The Sian Ka'an reserve is a natural reserve at the ocean with different lagunas where you can observe dolphins, turtles, birds, or just the beautiful water. However, if you want to do a trip in the reserve you have to reach deep into your pockets. An organized day trip to see the dolphins will cost you about 130 USD. Yes, crazy prices compared to the other activities in Mexico (except diving). There is another option to visit a small part of the reserve for much cheaper and it's possible to DIY. I'm talking about the channel float in Muyil.

What to expect of your visit to the Sian Ka'an reserve at Muyil

You will see beautiful, crystal clear green and blue water surrounded by mangroves. You will ride through this scenery for about one hour on a boat and in between, you will have your floating experience for about thirty minutes. This costs 600 pesos per person. They first wanted 700 pesos of us, but we knew that the going rate was 600 (which is too much if you ask me) and in the end, that's what we paid.

The Muyil ruins

To get to the shore of the laguna you can walk through a small archeological site. Although the ruins here were restored and not entirely original, the pyramids still looked cool.

The Muyil boardwalk and observatory

For 50 pesos you enter a wooden boardwalk and can climb up a hand-made-looking observatory to get a good view over the laguna. That was fun and exciting but it's just another stop in this tourist trap if you ask me.

The channel floating

That's probably what you have heard of and why you want to visit the reserve yourself. In the reserve, there are different channels between the mangroves. Some are manmade and some are natural. At high speeds, your boatman will ship you through the channels and across the laguna to bring you to a natural channel in which a slow but steady current pushes the freshwater toward the ocean. You are handed lifejackets which you can use to lie on or wear normally. However, they recommended to us to wear them like pampers, so that we'd float like corks.

The water is refreshing and can even become a bit cold since you can't get out of it until you reach the end of the floating after about 30 minutes. Therefore, be sure to only do it on a warm and sunny day. The clarity of the water is amazing and it's so peaceful to experience the serenity of nature while doing nothing but slowly being pushed along the channel. We didn't see anything but the mangroves, a few small fish, the sky, and sometimes the people from the group before or behind us.

My opinion of the channel floating

It was nice and special, but all is over within one and a half hours. For that, it's much too expensive. If 30 dollars for a boat ride without much to see but nice water and then the special experience of the floating are worth it to you, you find directions for the DIY trip below. Of course, if you compare it to the 130 USD of the organized tour, it's still cheap.

How to get from Tulum to Muyil and the Sian Ka'an floating

Take any ADO express going South and tell them that you want to get off at Muyil. This will cost about 30 pesos and the bus stop is 15 meters past the entrance to the small Muyil ruins.

There is a dirt road opposite the bus station that leads straight to the boat dock (10-min walk). By taking this path you don't have to pay the entrance fee to the ruins area.

One last tip: Don't take a colectivo to get to Muyil. The ride only takes 10 minutes and we paid 70 pesos per person. Plus, we first had to wait about 20 minutes until it was full). ADO or Mayab are the better options here. Mayab for sure will stop for you if you wave it down on your way back.

Mahaual

Traveling is also about embracing the unexpected and going with the flow. My plan for after Tulum was to first visit the natural reserve of Sian Ka'an at Muyil. Afterward, I wanted to continue to Bacalar. Little did I know in the morning that I would end up in the pretty coastal town of Mahaual.

As I was about to leave the kitchen after breakfast in Tulum, Pierre* from France overheard me talking that I was going to Bacalar. He asked if he could come along. Since it's always nicer to share a trip with someone and he was also down to make a stop at Muyil we were ready to go.

*I changed his name in this travel guide.

79

After the visit of the laguna and ruins in Muyil and having paid way too much for our colectivo to get there, I was getting more and more ready to try Pierre's idea of hitchhiking. He is an experienced hitchhiker. Since he was such a nice person, I thought that I could trust his instincts. Plus, it was bright daylight at the beginning of the afternoon.

Hitchhiking in Mexico

Pierre took out his sign and the erasable pen. He wrote Bacalar on the sign. We positioned ourselves right next to a dead snake along the road. That added even more to my nervosity. I never hitchhiked before. Was I crazy to do it in

Mexico? Even Mexicans in Europe had warned me that it was a dangerous country. Then again, I had only met the nicest people in Mexico so far- plus, I wasn't alone, and it was the middle of the day. These were the thoughts that went through my head as I was holding up the sign. I was hoping for two female tourists to stop. However, the first car that stopped contained two Mexican guys. Pierre said that one of them spoke good English and that they were ok to drive with. They were going to Mahaual but could at least bring us closer to Bacalar. So, after an introduction we were sitting on the back seat of a nice car with a/c, driving along with two Mexicans from Baja California. Soon I lost my last worries as they really were very nice.

Change of plans

They were telling us about Mahaual and how they ate one of the best grilled chickens in a roadside restaurant on the road to Mahaual, where they wanted to stop again if it was ok with us. By then, we had decided that we'd go to Mahaual with them. Of course, it was fine with us and half an hour later we were eating freshly (killed and) grilled chicken and sipping coconut water out of a coconut. The chicken really was good, and the funny thing was that the Mexicans were just as careful about possibly bad food as I was. But they trusted this restaurant.

With full stomachs, we continued to the small fishing village of Mahaual. I didn't think I would return to the coast again before flying back and was very happy that it worked out this way. If you want a few beach days, Mahaual is a great place to stay. There only is one road along which all the hotels and hostels are located and either you are directly at the beach or one street away from it.

Relaxing at the beach

We had a cerveza with our new friends and then set a date for the next day to go to Bacalar together as they were interested in seeing more of that area as well.

If you are tired of simply lying on the beach you can hop on a tourist boat and go snorkeling on the reef 10 min from shore. You will see lots of fish and turtles.
One of the people in our dorm went kite surfing, so that's also something you could do.

Tips for breakfast in Mahaual

There is a small place selling all kinds of fruit and vegetable juices for 13 pesos for half a liter. One crossroad away from it there is a French bakery with very affordable pastries and the Nutella croissant as well as the pain au chocolate are just delicious!!

Anyway, Mahaual is a nice spot to spend one or two days with direct beach access also for the lower budgets.

How to get to Mahahual without a rental car

Unfortunately, this is a bit more difficult, as ADO only has one connection per day to Mahahual. Either from Bacalar (1 h 20 mins, 90 pesos) or from Chetumal (1.5 h, 120 pesos). From both cities, however, there should be a colectivo at least every two hours, which costs similarly to the buses. In Mahahual, the colectivos wait at the football field (marked on Maps.me). In Chetumal and Bacalar you should ask the locals for the colectivos. To Chetumal, ADO buses depart every two hours from Tulum or vice versa (4h, with online discount about 200 pesos).

Lake Bacalar

Lake Bacalar somehow didn't cross the path of my travel research when I was home. So, I only learned about this gorgeous light blue lake when another traveler showed me pictures. I couldn't believe that that was a freshwater lake and not an ocean with such colors! I knew I had to adjust my schedule and also make a stop at Lake Bacalar - your budget version of the Maldives.

As usually on the Yucatan peninsula it's an advantage to have a car to drive around the lake area. Enough ADO buses go to Lake Bacalar, but the terminal is along the main road and you have to walk about 20 minutes to get to the lake.

What to do at Lake Bacalar

Enjoy the view of the Seven Colored Lagoon

There is a small fort from which you probably have an amazing view across all the different hues of the lagoon, but you also have a nice view from any spot directly along the water.

Take a bath in the laguna

There is one public beach a little to the left of the fort and otherwise, it's restaurants or beach clubs. We found our gem at 25 pesos on the lakeside close to the cenote (convenient if you have a car or bicycle, otherwise probably too far to walk). The beach club was called Cocalitos. Apart from that, I know that Yaxche Campground has a beach club as well to which you have access for free when you spend the night there.

Rent a kayak

It looks great when the colored kayaks glide across the blue water and it's fun to be able to go a little further out on the lake and see it from a different angle.

Take a boat tour

If you don't like to paddle yourself, you could do one of the many advertised tours. That was our initial plan, but we were so satisfied with our beach club that we didn't do one in the end.

Tip: Don't go to the cenote at Lake Bacalar

The cenote is just a big green creek that you probably can find enough of in your own country. It would be a waste of time you could better spend in and at Lake Bacalar.

Valladolid

In terms of nice colonial cities, people mostly mention Merida. However, I found Valladolid to be much more charming and easy to navigate. Here you find a few more reasons why you should spend at least a day and a night in the beautiful city of Valladolid.

- **Colorful houses**

Each street hides interesting gems as many houses are painted in different colors.

- **A beautiful church with a nice park**

Now, that's a nice park to sit and eat some churros in the evening. There are always vendors to get a dessert and I was lucky that they even had a live Salsa band on the first night I was there.

Eat delicious steak

Since food is cheaper here than on the coast, this city is a good place to eat steak arrachera which has melted cheese on top. Mine was simply delicious! Apart from that, you will find many good and affordable dishes inside the market hall opposite the main square.

- **Valladolid is the center of three main sights**

You can easily visit Chichen Itza, Rio Lagartos, and Ek Balam while being in Valladolid.

- **Cheap but great cenotes**

The cenotes, as well as the restaurants in this area, are cheaper but I actually found my favorite cenote in Valladolid.
There is a cenote in the center of town in Valladolid. It's called Zaci and only costs 35 pesos. It's a nice pool in a rocky cauldron where you can take a swim if you don't have time to drive out of town.

Hacienda Oxman

Cenote Oxman was my favorite cenote apart from Dos Ojos. It's possible to reach it in a half an hour bike ride or by car. The cenote is on a private property with a restaurant and a pool and therefore you better plan it in a way that you get to spend a few hours there to relax. For 80 pesos you can stay for the day and use lifejackets for free or jump from a rope. For 150 pesos you receive an additional drink, a snack, and the Wi-Fi password.

Oxman Cenote is nice from any angle. Whether you look from the top down into the crater or are inside along the brim or in the water below the vines, it's exactly that picturesque cenote you wished for. Another plus is that no tour bus stops here. Use maps.me to get there but only follow the big roads as they will be much easier to ride on than the dirt paths.

A taxi from Valladolid to get here costs about 100 pesos.

Xkeken and Samula Cenotes

This is a very touristic cenote that is often combined with the neighboring Samula one. It's a cenote inside a cave and if you haven't seen a cave cenote yet, this is a good one to go to at 80 pesos. However, if you have seen Dos Ojos, it won't impress you much. Same for Samula compared to Hacienda Oxman.

How to get to Valladolid

You can reach Valladolid by first- or second-class bus from Tulum in 1.5 hours starting at 81 pesos. From Cancun the bus trip takes about 2 h 15 mins, starting at 149 pesos. From Bacalar, the trip takes 4 hours and costs around 261 pesos. There aren't as many buses between Bacalar and Valladolid as between the other cities and you should ask at a station a few days ahead.

From Merida, you get to Valladolid in about 2.5 hours. There are frequent discounts online on the ADO website, starting at 142 pesos. Another option to travel between Merida and Valladolid is by colectivo. You can kill two birds with one stone by taking a colectivo to the yellow city of Izamal (read below) for 30 pesos. The drive takes 1.5 hours. Then, visit the city and afterward continue to Valladolid in 1h 40 minutes with *Autobuses Centro* for 70 pesos.

When traveling to Valladolid, keep the time difference in mind

Half of the year, Valladolid, Izamal, Merida, and Palenque are one hour behind the coastal cities and, therefore, you can sleep longer in case you travel from that direction :-). So, compare the time of Tulum and Valladolid before traveling there.

Izamal

This town is also called the yellow city as all the buildings are painted in a honey-colored yellow. Yes, ALL the buildings! The picturesque Mexican houses alone are inviting for a walk through the city, but you can also take great photos. The other good thing is, that it's a small town and you can visit everything on foot.

Half-day trip to Chichen Itza

Chichen Itza is one of the biggest archeological Mayan sites and, therefore, a must-visit on your trip to Mexico. They are located 45 minutes from Valladolid and can easily be visited by bus or colectivo. Try to catch the first colectivo in the morning. When you are there right when it opens at 8 a.m. you will be able to take some pictures without the tourist masses in the background.

How to get from Valladolid to Chichen Itza by public transport

I was blessed with jetlag throughout my whole vacation. "Blessed" because it woke me up around 6 a.m. which is great for having an early start to go exploring. So, it was an easy decision to get up for the first colectivo and I wasn't even surprised that the streets were completely deserted, since usually nothing is going on in Mexico before 8 a.m. The strange thing was, that there also wasn't any activity at the bus station when I got there. A kind man then pointed out to me that Valladolid is on central time and one hour behind Tulum time during the winter months. So, I actually had gotten up at 5.40 a.m. that morning without even feeling tired. But, oh well, I wrote some postcards and then walked toward the colectivo terminal again shortly before 7 a.m. That's when you should be there, too.

The colectivo terminal is located about 100 m before the ADO terminal toward the church. There was a guy (he is there all day) who calls out to all the passing people that the colectivo to Chichen Itza is leaving from here. Hence, you won't miss it. We waited 10 minutes until it was full and for 35 pesos, they brought us directly from Valladolid to Chichen Itza in one hour.

ADO only departs later and by then, hundreds of other tourists will have arrived. But perhaps you can use a bus on the way back as I bought a ticket from one of the chauffeurs and it cost only 30 pesos but was more comfortable than the colectivo.

Getting the ticket

Quickly get in line to buy the ticket. The entry price is 533 pesos for foreigners. Check their website (www.chichenitza.com/tickets) for a price update.

The pyramids

After entering through the main entrance, it's only a 3 min walk through the forest until you are standing in front of the impressive main pyramid. It's worth it to look at it from every side as all are different. I really liked the arena of the Mayan ball game as well and the pyramids near the second entrance.

In case you are tired of walking you can skip visiting the two cenotes. They are just dark green water holes and nothing special compared to the cenotes you can swim in. My visit took about 2 hours and 15 minutes with just walking everywhere, taking pictures, and reading some information panels. If you are there with a guide you will probably need longer.

Should I hire a guide to visit Chichen Itza?

If you have the time, I would say yes. I didn't have a guide, but I eavesdropped on some groups. Every time they were telling a really interesting story. So, here you will probably get good value for your money whereas in Tulum, I really didn't see the point in the guides since they only said what was already written on the info panel.

Facilities at Chichen Itza

Inside the park as well as outside there are many souvenir vendors. They actually could be haggled down to quite ok prices. I saw one snack bar inside the archeological site but there is a big restaurant and toilets at the entrance.

Day trip to Rio Lagartos and Ek Balam

Rio Lagartos is the town from which you start boat tours in the bio reserve where you can see pink lakes and flamingos. If you haven't yet seen the natural spectacle of a pink lake anywhere, don't miss this chance.

Ek Balam is a Mayan ruins city surrounded by a lush green forest. Exploring the ruins area makes you feel like Indiana Jones and the most awesome thing is that you can climb on the ruins. Even the very steep and high ones!

How to organize this day tour

First things first, if you have a car, you can easily combine Rio Lagartos and Ek Balam and even visit the cenote at Ek Balam in one day. Renting a car in Mexico is easy since there are many rental companies around and it's very common for tourists to rent a car. Prices for one day start as low as 15 USD!

By public transport, this amazing day trip is possible but stressful as there, unfortunately, isn't any direct connection to Ek Balam from Rio Lagartos. Therefore, I'd recommend planning one day for each of them if you don't have a car. Here is how you can fit both into one day anyway.

Or you could simply book a tour in Valladolid but going on your own gives you more freedom and will be cheaper.

From Valladolid to Rio Lagartos

Get one of the earliest possible buses from Valladolid to *Tizimin*. I left at 6.45 a.m. with Oriente Express for 30 pesos and the journey took about one hour.

Tizimin is a lively town that has quite a few small food options around the station, but I was only interested in how to get to Rio Lagartos as quickly as possible. Unfortunately, there are very few buses going there and so you have to ask for the colectivos that are situated one block to the right from the bus station. It just so happened that 3 people in a yellow taxi were looking to go to Rio Lagartos and since the taxi was full with me, off we were on the 45-minute ride. It cost 50 pesos. Just as much as the normal colectivo.

Boat tour at Rio Lagartos

I was hoping that I could join other people for a boat tour once I arrived there. You can haggle it down to 500 pesos if you are on your own. 200 per person if you are four people. However, I was the only tourist along the water. Unfortunately, the other tourists that were arriving had already booked a complete tour and therefore didn't have any interest in taking me with them. Hence, it's better if you are several people for this trip.

At least the harbor workers were very nice. One of them organized that I could join an organized group tour in about 50 minutes. In the meantime, they brought me to a place where I could eat some empanadas.

2-hour boat tour at Rio Lagartos

Finally, I could hop onto the small longboat that had space for about 8 people. I was joined by a Chinese family from North Carolina and their guide. Luckily, our boat had a sun protection roof unlike most of the other boats. Our captain also brought a few dead fish aboard that he later fed to the pelicans.

The tour starts with a 45-minute ride through a nice green scenery up the river. We made stops to take pictures of different birds. Sometimes you are also lucky enough to see a crocodile, but we didn't see one.

The next stop is a little further up the river and you might already see the pink hue on the horizon. Or you might smell the flamingos that live up here and it's cool to see them in the wilderness! The captain said that they are pink because they eat a certain kind of algae that grows here. This brings me to the next highlight on the tour.

The pink lake at Rio Lagartos

Behind a sand well the water suddenly is not green anymore but a red-brown and if the sun shines directly into it it's really pink!

In the background, you can see the saline. They have built the water channels in a way that they never dry out where the algae are but can evaporate where they are gaining the salt. It was pretty neat to see such a vast area of water being pink and that having happened naturally.

The Mayan mud bath

Our captain took a bucket of mud/sand out of the green side of the river and then we started our journey back to the marina. Most people put the mud on their arms and face on the boat ride back, so that it can dry for 15 minutes. Then, they'd wash it off at the beach at the open sea a little past the marina where we got on in the morning. However, we covered our whole bodies once we reached the white beach and then hung out there for a few minutes until the mud was dry, upon which we washed it off again in the seawater.

The complete tour took 2 hours and was a much better value than the one in Muyil.

How to get from Rio Lagartos to Ek Balam

Now it was already 12.45 p.m. They told me the next colectivo to Tizimin would leave at 1.20 p.m. but in the end, we drove around town a few times until the colectivo filled up and it was 1.45. Ek Balam is only open until 5 p.m. and, therefore, it would be a bit of a close call. I tried it, nevertheless.

From Tizimin to Ek Balam

Even after speaking to several people the answer still remained the same. I would have to return to Valladolid and then get another colectivo from there to the ruins. But I'd lose at least an hour through that and then the ruins would be closed for sure.

Finally, a driver of a yellow colectivo taxi brought me to the crossroad to Ek Balam for 35 pesos. From there it would be 7 km to the ruins and colectivos should stop along the road to take me there. So, I started walking but nobody stopped! That got quite depressing after a while since it was getting close to 4 p.m. and it was hot as hell as well. Probably it was too late for colectivos heading this direction at this time of day and therefore, I really can't recommend doing this part of the excursion the way I did it. Luckily, there were some friendly locals who picked me up and brought me to the parking lot of the ruins.

The ruins at Ek Balam

Fortunately, I still had one hour to visit them. The site is not big and so that was just enough, but 1.5 hours would have been better. The best thing was that there were hardly any tourists left in the park. Plus, everything looked really nice in the soft light of late afternoon.

Climbing the pyramids

The cool thing about Ek Balam is that you can climb on the pyramids. It gave me a little vertigo going up and down the steep steps. However, the view over the jungle and the other pyramids is amazing! In addition, the main pyramid was very nicely ornamented. It really is a work of art.

Visiting Ek Balam

The entry fee is 413 pesos. If you want to have an easy trip by public transport, take the ADO bus leaving Valladolid at 8 a.m. It Returns at 12 for 80 pesos roundtrip.

One mile from the ruins you find *X'Canche* Cenote. It is in an open crater and a waterfall falls into the cenote. Therefore, X'Canche is worth visiting as well. The entry fee is 70 pesos and if you want a taxi ride to and from the centoe it costs 150 pesos including the entry fee.

I was lucky that there were three French girls at Ek Balam who also traveled by colectivo. So, we could head back to Valladolid together for 50 pesos per person.

It was a long day with many impressions but it's definitely worth visiting both Rio Lagartos and Ek Balam. Yet, if you have enough time, do it in two days (if you don't have a car). Rather relax at a cenote in Valladolid for the rest of the day.

Merida

Merida is the capital of the Yucatan state. This city welcomed me with a dry heat of 40 degrees. Therefore, forget to explore the city between 1 p.m. and 4.30 p.m. and look for a hotel or hostel with a pool where you can rest.

There certainly are pretty, colorful houses in Merida and if you want to stretch your legs in the shade of trees, stroll along Paseo Montejo. However, the city is too big to see all its corners on foot and it didn't have a center of ambiance like Valladolid. Also, I wasn't impressed by any of the markets in Merida. This city rather seems to be a big hub where you don't necessarily have to spend a night.
Yet, if you are looking for some suggestions for what to do in Merida, here is what you can do:

Watch a spectacle

At 8 p.m. there was an outdoor theater at the main square with folkloric dances and actors. You can buy a ticket to watch it from up close or you can watch from further away from behind the fence.

Watch Aztecan football

If you have visited any big ruins in Mexico, you will have heard about Pok ta Pok, a ball game where the players had to get a ball into a stone ring that was attached high up on a wall. The winner then was sacrificed to the Gods, which was a big honor.
Before Covid, every Friday evening, a Pok ta Pok game was re-enacted on Plaza Grande in front of Merida Cathedral. I

would have loved to see that, and I hope they will pick this tradition up again, once things with the virus get better.

Have a Margarita

Of course, you will have many chances in Mexico to drink a good Margarita. However, in many hostels or cheap bars, they are watered down. Unlike at *Los Trompos Taqueria* where I had an absolutely delicious Margarita for 35 pesos and the guacamole was very good as well.

Go to the beach

The pretty beach town of *Progreso* is only 50 minutes away by bus (20 pesos). The buses leave frequently from the AutoProgreso station.

Swim in a cenote

Honesty, I liked the cenotes around Tulum and Valladolid better than the ones in the Merida area because they had more variety. However, if this is your only chance to see cenotes, it will still be worth the trip as you can find cave cenotes with the typical clear blue water in the town of *Homun*.

How to get to Homun

Take a colectivo to Homun for 23 pesos one way. It takes a little over an hour, but you might have to wait a bit until the colectivo is filled. There are more than 30 cenotes near Homun. Guides will want to offer you their services and chauffeur you around in their tuk-tuks. However, they will only bring you to the cenotes within walking distance anyway, so you might as well walk there without paying for a guide.

We visited *Tza Ujun Kat* Cenote Which was a big cave with a round opening in the center, where they planted plants. The cenote next to it was very small but also with a steep descent downstairs into the cenote.

We had to rent lifejackets since they said wearing them was obligatory. We got them for the day at the rental place at the parking lot. However, they didn't check all the time whether we were wearing them, so to save some money you might want to split one lifejacket between two people. If they have a security guard, you just can't be in the water at the same time.

The biggest cenote of those three in that area is Santa Rosa.
All cenotes cost 50 pesos to enter but since they are so similar, just going to one or two might be enough. Yet still a lot cheaper than the cenotes near Tulum.

Another famous cenote in this area is Cuzama. However, it turned into a tourist spectacle. Carts drawn by ill-looking horses will bring you to the entrance of the cenote. Therefore, it's better that you don't go there and don't support this animal maltreatment.

Uxmal ruins

If you haven't been to Chichen Itza, the Uxmal ruins are a good alternative. They are certainly pretty and very well preserved (especially the ball arena). Plus, without Covid regulations, you can climb the Uxmal ruins which you can't in Chichen Itza and there are hardly any tourists at Uxmal. However, Uxmal is just as expensive at 430 pesos.

When you are traveling in Mexico for a while, you will realize just how many amazing archeological sites you could visit and for every ruin you visit you will learn about another one nearby. Mostly, the lesser-known ones also cost a lot less but that doesn't mean that they aren't as great as the expensive ones. You won't be able to visit them all. Therefore, take your pick and make some cuts.

You can easily reach Uxmal from the bus station next to the ADO station. The journey takes one hour and costs 60 pesos. The times change and perhaps you can ask the evening before about when the buses are leaving. Usually, there are two buses in the morning. Alternatively, there are also two colectivos in the morning which also depart from in front of the same bus station for 65 pesos one way. To return to Merida you wait on the opposite side of the road and flag down a bus.

Where to stay in Merida

Apart from the city not really having too many attractions, the pretty hotels in Merida are the attractions themselves. If you pay a bit more, you can stay in beautiful colonial-style boutique hotels with colorful walls, pretty arches, and local plants. For example:

Viva Merida Hotel Boutique

Viva Merida Hotel Boutique (www.vivameridahotel. com/galeria) is designed in a very instagramable Mexican colonial style. The hotel is clean, and I slept in a big, comfy four-poster bed. Since the ceiling is so high, my room spread over two stories and I felt like I had a whole apartment to myself. There is a small pool where you can cool off during the hottest hours of the day. Plus, the staff is very friendly and helpful!

Leaving Merida

You can head to Valladolid in 2 h 15 mins by ADO for 260 pesos.
Another popular trip is the journey to Campeche (which, by the way, you can also reach directly from Uxmal). I haven't found any colectivos, but different bus classes leave from

the ADO terminal. The direct ADO buses leave hourly, cost about 260 pesos, and take 2 hours. If you want it cheaper, ask for "el bus mas barato a Campeche". The cheaper buses leave a bit less frequently. Unfortunately, there aren't any timetables, and you have to ask at the station. I went with ATS at 11 a.m. for 190 pesos. The journey took 3h 20 mins.

You can also head directly from Merida to Palenque. The bus ride takes 9 hours, leads via Campeche, and costs 822 pesos.

Merida to Cancun takes 4 hours and costs 506 pesos.

Campeche

This town hosts lots of pretty, colorful buildings, even more than in Merida. On top of that, it's located by the ocean which would give this town a huge potential to become a tourist hotspot.

Unfortunately, the advantages of Campeche aren't used beneficially and there is not really a nice hostel to stay at (there were only two places to choose from). Therefore, I'd recommend only spending a couple of hours in Campeche and then leaving again. To get to Palenque, there only are two night buses anyway (and one day bus, that leaves at 11 a. m.), so you could spend the day in Campeche and leave in the evening.

The ADO bus station of Campeche is outside the historic city center. You can take any public bus along the main road for 7 pesos to get to the market, which is just outside the city walls of the historical part.

What to do in Campeche

You can have a drink at *Calle 59* which is very touristy and has many bars. Then, you could stroll along the *Malecón*, which is a long promenade on the seafront with statues and outdoor workout stations. However, the water is dirty with garbage floating around, and if you are looking for a place where you can enter the water and swim you will search in vain. Believe me, I have tried. I even accompanied two friends in their car to explore the coast North of Campeche up to Sebaplaya and in the end, we had to give up and return to Campeche without swimming. All the beaches we encountered were so dirty, that you'd probably catch an incurable disease. The only beach that looked nice with white sand and palm trees was Playa Bonita, which can be reached in 30 minutes by colectivo from opposite the market. You need to get a ride to Lerma (7 pesos) and ask them about Playa Bonita.

However, due to Covid, you could only enter the private beach of the restaurant and because they were just packing up as we arrived, we weren't allowed to enter anymore. In summary, don't come to Campeche if you want to go swimming or visit a beach. There are much better places for this in Mexico.

Oh well, back in Campeche we had a nice seafood dinner while watching the sunset at La *Palapa del Tio Fito*. That seems to be a popular dinner spot. The food was good but prices a bit more elevated at 10 to 15 USD per main dish.

After sunset, you could stroll through *Parque Moch Cohuho* to the left of the angel monument. Some bridges in the park are illuminated at night, which looks nice. In addition, there is a fountain show with lights and music at 8 p. m. in front of that park in *Parque de las Puertas*. Be careful, if the wind blows inland, you will be soaked very quickly. But that's where the touristy bit ends. Although Campeche has all these facilities, it somehow feels like this place is not really ready for tourists. For example, the market is big, overwhelming and you can't find fresh fruit juice anywhere. Only fruit water and perhaps pre-made orange juice. On top of that, there is a constant mixture of odd smells since bloody animals are lying on the stands next to clothes and vegetables. Where is the system in this market? Yet, you should try something with "conchinita". It is pulled pork and whatever dish you choose (taco, torta (sandwich), etc.) will be very delicious.

Insider tip: In case your hair could use a cut, look for the "calle peluqueria" behind the market on the way to the colectivos to the Edzna ruins. A simple cut without a massage and washing costs 25 pesos only. It's nothing fancy, but great if you want to get rid of unhealthy split ends.

Half-day trip to the Edzna Ruins

My reason for coming to Campeche (apart from having read that there are colorful houses) was, that it's easy to get to the Edzna Ruins from Campeche. It's an archeological site with one big temple, a long gallery, and a few smaller pyramids. So, not a big ancient city but what is amazing about Edzna is that it's located in a lush green jungle and even now, during Covid, we were allowed to climb to the top of the pyramids!

Red and white colectivo vans leave Campeche hourly at '30. Since it was raining that day, I was in no hurry to get up and took the colectivo at 10.30 a.m. The spot is marked on maps.me. The drive to the ruins took 1 hour and cost 45 pesos. They dropped me off at the parking lot and told me that a colectivo back to Campeche would come back every hour.

By now, the sun was back out and there was no sign that it had rained in the morning. The entrance fee was 65 pesos. I only had 500 pesos and they couldn't give me any change because there hadn't been enough other visitors yet. They told me, I should come back at the end of my visit and pay then.

First, you then enter a small museum hut with a few archeological display items. Afterward, you walk 300 m through the forest until you see the ruins spreading across the grass. There is one big temple and a long wall with stairs. For now, only two other tourists were present and for about half an hour I had the whole temple to myself and enjoyed climbing the smaller pyramids around the big Acropolis.

With taking a break on top of one of the pyramids I was done with my tour in 90 minutes. By then, some more people had arrived and I could pay for my ticket.

Unfortunately, I then just missed the colectivo to Campeche and so I waited in the shade of a tree. When still no colectivo came after over an hour, I walked to the road to wait there. Maybe I should have done that from the beginning since more colectivos were driving along that road. Probably, not all of them come to the parking lot.

Once more, I found myself waiting in the searing sun next to a Mexican highway. I never found out how much later the next colectivo arrived because two tourists picked me up a little later and gave me a ride back to Campeche. Thank you again for that :-).

Palenque

Already during my first trip to Mexico, I wanted to visit Palenque. I had heard a lot about this small town in the lush jungle with ruins that you can climb and waterfalls so blue that you think they colored them. However, I underestimated the distances in the Yucatan area. Palenque is in a different state than Merida or Cancun and it takes some effort to get there. However, the waterfalls really are amazing, and I am glad that, with some planning, I managed to include Palenque on my second trip.

How to get to Palenque

By plane

There actually is an airport a few kilometers from Palenque, but it wasn't operating. Perhaps it's because of Covid. Anyway, it would be very convenient if you could fly directly to Palenque and therefore, it's worth checking whether there are any changes with the Palenque airport. Now, if you want to arrive or leave by plane, you have to fly to Villahermosa. You can travel between Palenque airport and Villahermosa by colectivo or ADO bus. The ADO buses generally cost 350 pesos. I thought it would be more reliable to just go with ADO, in order to reach the airport on time. But then, my ADO bus at 5 p.m. was canceled at 5.05 p.m. and I was left looking for a colectivo after all. There are three colectivo companies which are located between the big roundabout at the ADO station and the hospital. The first one cost 150 pesos (van), the second one 250 pesos (taxi), and Jaguar Transporte (at the top of Hidalgo Huerta Street, 5 minutes walking from the others) cost 200 pesos. I went with them because they all only leave when they are full and most people were waiting at Jaguar.

If you take a transport into Villahermosa downtown, it would be cheaper. Perhaps, from there, it would also cost less to get to the airport. So, if you have enough time, you could take a detour via Villahermosa city.

By bus from Merida or Campeche

By bus, you can reach Palenque from Merida (9 hours, 822 pesos). The same bus leaves Campeche 2.5 hours later. If you check ahead online, you might get a discount. My bus from Campeche to Palenque at 00.50 left on time. I had a discounted price because I bought it online on the ADO website for 300 pesos instead of 542 pesos. The journey takes 6 hours.

By colectivo to San Cristobal de las Casas

Another popular connection is to go to (or come from) San Cristobal de las Casas. That stretch of road was the only one about which I read some danger warnings. Therefore (and because I had no time left), I didn't travel this way on this trip. However, no other traveler that came from that direction told me they had seen or felt anything strange. Also, I heard that in a tour van you should be safe from the gangs that sometimes rob the buses. So, perhaps ask the locals before organizing your trip between San Cristobal and Palenque whether the road is safe at the moment. The travelers I have spoken to had booked a waterfall tour with direct transport. It cost the same as if they had returned to their original city.

If joining a waterfall tour and switching to the next town on the same day seems too stressful to you, you could take the public colectivos on another day. First, you travel to Ocosingo (the same colectivo would drop you off at Misol-Ha or Agua Azul) and then another one to San Cristobal. Each colectivo costs 90 pesos. The journey without any waterfall stops takes 5 hours.

ADO takes a safer route via Villahermosa and Tuxtla. The journey takes 9 hours and costs 380 pesos.

What to do in Palenque

If you opt for accommodation in the jungle, you should spend some time simply listening to the sounds of the monkeys and other animals. If you stay in the city center, you should take a walk along the road, where the market is located. The whole street is very busy with vendors and has a nice, local feel to it.

How to visit the Palenque Ruins

You can easily visit the ruins by taking a colectivo from the main roundabout in the village center. They leave every 10 minutes, take 15 minutes to get to the ruins, and cost 20 pesos. The entrance fee is 37 pesos for the national park and 80 pesos for the ruins.

This gives you the freedom to stay as long or short as you please.

However, if you also want to visit Misol-Ha and Agua Azul waterfalls, a tour will include less hassle and might even work out cheaper.

Tour of the Palenque ruins, Misol-Ha, and Agua Azul

I arrived with my night bus on time in Palenque early in the morning. Directly at the ADO station, a guy wanted to sell me the waterfall tour for 570 pesos. In front of the station was *Tulum Transporte*, they offered the tour for 510 pesos.

Hence, it's really easy to find a tour for the same day when you arrive by night bus. Tulum Transporte had different starting times. If you start later, you will have less time at the ruins, but for me, that was no problem, as two hours were enough for the ruins and a walk in the jungle (without a guided tour and without being able to climb the ruins, due to Covid restrictions).

You might save 50-100 pesos if you do the whole tour on your own in one day by catching different colectivos toward Misol-Ha and Agua Azul. However, you will have to walk from the main road to Misol-Ha and might have long waiting times until the next colectivo picks you up. Hence, it's a lot easier to just hop on and off the tour van.

My tour with Tulum Transporte

They picked me up at my hostel right on time at 9 a.m. We first brought another couple to the zoo and then continued to the ruins. Unfortunately, a lot was closed in the ruins area due to Covid and you couldn't climb any ruins or go to the waterfall at the back. This was disappointing since I had been looking forward to exploring those ruins for years. Only looking at them from the ground didn't make them more special than other ruins. For example, the Ek Balam or Coba ruins also have a jungle feel to them but are a lot easier accessible from Valladolid than traveling all the way to Palenque just for the ruins.

I was finished with my visit in one hour but then had to wait 2 hours for my tour van to come again. I passed the time by drinking and eating a coconut (20 pesos) and taking a walk through the rainforest on the official path. The round trip takes about 40 minutes. If you go with a guide, it will take a bit longer. There actually would be many more ruins in the jungle. Only a small part is excavated. However, the government doesn't have any money to work on the ruins that are still covered.

Misol-Ha

Our van showed up at 12.20 p.m. and we drove to Misol-Ha waterfall in 30 minutes (entry fee without the tour: 30

pesos). For this strong single-stream waterfall, we only received 30 minutes, but I could have easily stayed longer! We should have cut time at the ruins and spent more time here. You could walk behind the waterfall and take showers in smaller streams. Plus, there were black monkeys in the trees, and it was entertaining to watch them. Swimming in the pond didn't look so inviting and even a bit dangerous, but it's possible because a guy was handing out lifejackets.

Agua Azul

Due to many stops because of construction work, we finally reached Agua Azul 1.5 hours later (entry fee without the tour: 50 pesos). Now, this sightseeing spot didn't disappoint! We saw the water shining blue through the trees as soon as we arrived. It's not just one waterfall but you can follow the water along the river and discover smaller ponds and waterfalls.

I had been unlucky in Asia many times where supposedly blue waterfalls were a muddy brown but here at Agua Azul, I caught a picture-perfect day at the end of the dry season. However, don't come in the rainy season. Then, the high waters turn into a muddy brown as well.

Agua Azul is very touristy and the whole area along the river is covered with restaurants. So, after taking pictures and swimming in some of the ponds you can fill your hungry belly with some empanadas or enjoy a drink with a view of the waterfall.

Returning to Palenque

I only got dropped off at my hostel at 7.30 p. m. since we waited for 15 minutes en route until a crossing van arrived that would bring some of our passengers directly to San Cristobal de las Casas. As already mentioned, combining the tour with the trip west would be a good option if you want to head in that direction.

Back in Palenque we first dropped off all the people in the hotels in the jungle. By then, I was asking myself again why I had joined a tour. I probably wasted just as much time today by being slowed down through the tour as I would have been by traveling on colectivos and foot. Yet, we saw a lot in one day and all the organization worked out well.

Cascada Roberto Barrios

While visiting the other sights in Palenque, several times Roberto Barrios waterfall was mentioned to me. Therefore, I made my way there the next day, and, boy, am I happy that I did!

To get to the town of Roberto Barrios, take a colectivo van in Palenque from a road near the central market. The spot is marked on maps.me. They leave all the time when they are full. The ride costs 50 pesos and takes 50 minutes to the small pueblo of Roberto Barrios.

At the final stop of the colectivo you pay an entrance fee to the waterfall (30 pesos). Then, you walk along a stone path for 200 m (which feels much longer in the sun) until you arrive at the river in the cooling forest. The main bathing pools are downstream to the left side, but the river also looks nice to the right side. It's possible to swim there too.

The color of the water was very beautiful, and it flowed over many rock pools. It was difficult to pick the most beautiful spot for swimming as everything was so nice.

I would say, this place wins over Agua Azul because it's less touristy and a lot easier to reach from Palenque. You could stay the whole day at Roberto Barrios or just a couple of hours. In the wet season, there will be a lot more water here. It might be too dangerous to swim then. Better ask the locals before you go.

It's definitely possible to visit Roberto Barrios during the day and then take a flight from Villahermosa in the evening.

Experiences as a solo female traveler in Mexico

I travel solo a lot but mostly in Southeast Asia where I've found it not to be an issue at all. Before my first trip to Mexico, I hadn't been to Latin America except for when I visited a friend in Honduras. So, going to Mexico as a solo female traveler was a new experience and I wasn't sure whether I would like it or whether I'd feel safe. Mostly, because my Mexican friends in Switzerland gave me all these security tips beforehand. Would it really be so dangerous? I extra picked the Yucatan area as my first destination because I knew that it would be very touristy and probably only the "Mexico light" version. If I'd like it, I'd come back for more. So, what did I think of Mexico as a solo female traveler?

My general opinion of traveling in Mexico as a solo female traveler

I loved the Yucatan region! The beaches are like paradise, the water of the ocean, the cenotes or lakes is crystal clear, the food is delicious, and generally, people are very nice and helpful. Obviously, I had to return and see more of Mexico.

Did I ever feel unsafe?

Yes, while walking along highways and roads. People drive fast, talk on the phone while driving, and it's never clear who has the right of going first. Plus, not even on Bali have I seen so many tourists with injuries from scooter accidents like here in Mexico. I'd stay away from the scooters and just always be cautious along roads if I were you.

Also, Mexican guys can be a bit annoying with not understanding that I'm not interested in them. It also doesn't interest them that I have a boyfriend. "You can have several", was their answer. I tried to never end up alone with them. But, of course, not all guys were like that. Again, there also were some real gentlemen.

Is it safe to arrive somewhere late at night?

In tourist places, I would say yes. Cancun and Playa del Carmen are party cities and there will be many people out and about. In Mexico City, you just order a trackable cab and head directly to your accommodation.

Did I ever feel lonely?

During all my time in Mexico (pre-covid and during covid) it was very easy to spike up a conversation with anyone. I made friends at the beach, at hostels, in bars, and at restaurants. People are friendly and also prefer to share stories and meet different people. If you are a bit open yourself it will be easy to connect.

I did feel lonely once though because I ended up in a dorm with no other people. It was nice to have a room to myself for once but on the other hand, I didn't get the chance to make plans for the next day (which was going to the remote area in beautiful Rio Lagartos). I talked to many people as well that day, but the contacts were always so short that the experience didn't really feel shared.

My tips for a solo female traveler in Mexico

Just behave as cautious as your instincts tell you. If you feel at ease, your feeling is probably right. If you are worried, try to get out of the situation or find a friendly-looking person and just talk to them.

Don't walk alone in dark alleys at night, you know, the usual thing... Most important, don't let anyone stop you from traveling to Mexico just because nobody is coming with you. You will have an amazing time!

Some useful words in Spanish

English	Spanish
Hello	Hola
How are you?	¿Cómo estás?
I'm well and you?	Bien, gracias y tú?
Where are you from?	¿De donde eres?
I'm from...	Soy de..(Estados Unidos, Inglaterra)
Yes	Si
No	No
Where is the toilet/ATM?	¿Dónde está el baño/cajero?
Thank you.	Gracias
How much is...?	¿Cuánto cuesta...?
Sorry	Lo siento
Please	Por favor
I need to change money.	Necesito cambiar dinero.
I would like...	Me gustaría... / Quiero...
The bill please.	La cuenta, por favor.
Water	Agua
Chicken	Pollo
Without meat	Sin carne
Enjoy your meal.	Buen provecho.
What time does... arrive?	¿Cuándo llegará...?
Bus	El autobús
Plane	El avión
Boat	El barco
Waterfall	La cascada
Right	Derecha
Left	Izquierda

About the author of this travel guide

Seraina loves to travel since she can remember. It started with beach vacations with her family when she was a child but soon, she sought her own routes. She was lucky to be able to spend an amazing High School year in New York at 15 years old. That's when she started to write her first travel blog which evolved into SwissMissOnTour (www.swissmissontour.com). Later, she explored Europe with Interrail but was also attracted by the exotic countries further away. Countless trips to South East Asia made her fall in love with the delicious Asian flavors, beautiful temples, and natural highlights. South America was always at the back of her mind but for that, she wanted to have more time in order not to have to fly back and forth to Switzerland in every vacation. So, when the timing was right, she quit her job and was fully enjoying the countries of Central and South America. Covid then made her trip come to a full stop. Until border openings are reliable again, she is back in Switzerland, taking every opportunity she gets to see more of Switzerland and the world.

Do you need more info?

In case you need more info, I am happy to help. Contact or follow me through these channels:

(b) www.swissmissontour.com

(i) @swissmissontour

(f) SwissMissOnTour

(w) www.slgigerbooks.wordpress.com

By the way, since the photos in this travel guide are black and white, you can send me an e-mail with a picture of the book and I will send you the e-book version of I love Mexico for free. In the e-book, the pictures are in color.

Did you like this travel guide?

In case you liked this travel guide, I'd greatly appreciate a positive review on Amazon, and it would be a good support if you told your friends about it 😊

More books by S. L. Giger

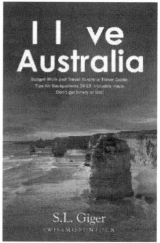

Printed in Great Britain
by Amazon